# THE NEW SPOON RIVER

# THE NEW
# SPOON RIVER

B Y

Edgar Lee Masters

❦

INTRODUCTION BY *Willis Barnstone*

*THE MACMILLAN COMPANY, NEW YORK, NEW YORK*

Grateful acknowledgment is given to the following publishers for permission to reprint previously published material: Bantam Books, Inc., for lines from *Greek Lyric Poetry*, translated by Willis Barnstone, copyright © 1962 by Bantam Books, Inc., Liveright Publishing Company for lines from "The River" in *Complete Poems & Prose of Hart Crane* © 1933; Longmans, Green & Company Ltd. for lines from *Select Epigrams from the Greek Anthology* by J. W. Mackail.

Library of Congress Catalog Card Number: 68–14440

FOURTH PRINTING 1971

*The Macmillan Company*
*866 Third Avenue, New York, N.Y. 10022*

Printed in the United States of America

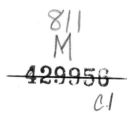

"Tragedy as it was antiently compos'd, hath ever been held the gravest, moralest and most profitable of all other poems: therefore said by Aristotle to be of power . . . to purge the mind of those and such like passions. Nor is Nature wanting in her own effects to make good his assertion: for so in physics things of melancholic hue and quality are us'd against melancholy, sour against sour, salt to remove salt humour."
—MILTON

"The irony I invoke is no cruel deity. She mocks neither love nor beauty."
—ANATOLE FRANCE

# CONTENTS

# CONTENTS

CONTENTS

# CONTENTS

CONTENTS

CONTENTS

# CONTENTS

CONTENTS

CONTENTS

xvi

# INTRODUCTION

When *Spoon River Anthology* first appeared in 1915, it was greeted as a new form of literary expression and as a breakthrough in its candid treatment of small-town mores. It received phenomenal public acclaim, greater than any volume of poems since *Hiawatha*. Yet, because of its exposure of rural life, it also provoked a nationwide moral controversy.[1] Looking back, it is strange to recall how once an angry young man's poems could have so pleased and outraged an American public, how Edgar Lee Masters' verbal missiles against a philistine target achieved such a noisy success. By 1961 *Spoon River Anthology* had gone through seventy editions, had been translated into at least eight foreign tongues, and had been made into an American play and an Italian opera, which was sung at La Scala.

Today, however, it is necessary to redeem the *Anthology*, to argue, ironically, that *despite* its great popular success in the past (for standards we may now reject) it is a superior work—in advance of its time—and demands critical reappraisal. In reality, the confessional monologues of tragic existences in both *Spoon River Anthology* (1915) and its continuation, *The New Spoon River* (1924), are closer to the worlds of Theodore Roethke, Robert Lowell, and Sylvia Plath than to poems by any of Masters' contemporaries. In their fresh, rough diction, in their uncompromisingly irrever-

---

[1] For a summary of the initial response to *Spoon River Anthology*, see Percy H. Boynton, "The Voice of Chicago—Edgar Lee Masters and Carl Sandburg," in *Some Contemporary Americans* (Chicago, 1924), pp. 52–53, and Lois Hartley, *Spoon River Revisited*, Ball State Monograph Number One (Muncie, Indiana, [n.d.]), pp. 3–5.

ent and dark mood, in their poetic exploitation of the common and banal, Masters' poems anticipate the work of our best poets in the post-World War II era.

Masters was a Midwesterner. With Vachel Lindsay and Carl Sandburg, he was in the vanguard of the poetic renaissance that made Chicago and the Middle West a pivotal force in American poetry. Born in Garnett, Kansas, in 1869, he spent his childhood and youth in the Illinois towns of Petersburg and Lewistown. These two rural communities were to be the source of many of his poems. He studied Greek for a year at Knox College, and became a Chicago lawyer, an activist in Popularist movements, and a writer. When *Spoon River* appeared in 1915, the time was right. In the American village and city his targets of narrow morality, hypocrisy, shabby injustice, fat complacency, and inelegant materialism were in full view. The *new morality* we speak of today—although, of course, in different forms—was just then being discovered. The popularist, anarchist, social reformer, novelist, and poet were holding an old fabric of personal and public morality up to light, to see only a threadbare rag with faded colors.

By 1924, when *The New Spoon River* appeared, Masters' social message had already made its greatest impact, and its novelty and shock value were gone. This book was also a bestseller, but only a qualified literary success. In general critics then and now have considered the second *Spoon River* a secondary achievement. Critical evaluation of both volumes, however, has been unduly limited to assessment of Masters' literary originality and of his social ideas.

The social circumstances that contributed to the *succès de scandale* of both volumes are important to literary history; but they are largely irrelevant to evaluation of the books as works of literary art. Yet qualities beyond social journalism and literary history redeem this often graceless miscellany of dramatic monologues. More than his anger, his outrage before cant, his cranky politics, his radicalism today not so radical, Masters may be seen for his profound empathy with shattered lives, for his relentless preoccupation with the tragic limitations of small and great people. More important than his questioning of the old and new moralities is his revelation of the people who were victims of these moralities, of those inhabitants of Spoon River who were tragically obsessed with impossible ideals or flawed with every form of human corruption. Masters' pessimism is absolute; often, at his best, almost unbearable. Like those epitaphs that he paraphrases from the Greek Anthology, he aspires to a bit of sweet sunlight; but light and darkness are all, and the tomb—before enough light has been sucked in—prevails. In depicting a doomed world, crossed here and there by quick rays of sun, Masters—in the parabolic manner of Franz Kafka and Constantine Cavafy—placed his personages behind huge walls, from which death was the only apparent escape. Yet even death did not silence them. From the cemetery hill, his figures continued to speak of their frustrations and failures, of the insanity, murders, and diseases that are the themes of their epitaphs.

How did Masters come upon the unique structure for the *Anthology?* In his autobiography, *Across Spoon River* (1924), he wrote that he had originally planned to write an extended work in prose. Then one day in 1913, William M. Reedy, editor of *Reedy's Mirror* to which Masters had frequently contributed poems, gave him a copy of the second edition of J. W. Mackail's *Select Epigrams from the Greek Anthology* (1906). The effect of the Greek Anthology upon Masters' own work has never been properly studied. Very much of the mood and form of *Spoon River* may be traced directly to the Greek Anthology.

The Greek or Palatine Anthology is a collection of some four thousand short poems—largely epigrams—dating from 700 B.C. to A.D. 1000, from Archilochos to the late Byzantine Christian apologists. Most of the poems are about people— brief striking biographies—and, like Masters' epitaphs, spoken in the first person singular. It contains poems that are amazingly objective, frank about every kind of sexual activity; it contains lampoons and bitterly tragic complaints. As in Masters, there is sun and darkness—and more darkness than sun—and apart from the Byzantine Christian epigrams (which are a late and inferior addition), there is little hope

_₤ salvation. Love and humor and fearful death dominate the collection.

Masters made use of the Greek Anthology in several ways. Above all, he obtained from the Anthology—as his own title suggests—the concept of the *anthology,* the basic unifying device in his work. In Greek an *anthologia* is a gathering of flowers, that is, a collection of choice related lyrics. The word anthology is first associated with the Greek Anthology. Meleagros, the first compiler of the Greek Anthology, also called the collection his *stephanos*: a garland or wreath of flowers. The lyrics hang together because of similarities in structure and theme.

It is impossible in one long, unbroken poem to remain evenly upon a summit of lyrical ecstasy. The device of an anthology or a sequence of short related poems is Masters' solution to the esthetic problem of how to extend the lyric voice successfully beyond Poe's forbidding one-hundred-line barrier: how to write a long lyric poem without lapsing into narrative or descending into boredom. Other writers have also resorted to a *sequence* of connecting lyrics in order to give both unity and extension to their efforts: Rilke in his *Sonnets to Orpheus;* García Lorca in *Cante jondo* and *Romancero gitano;* Meredith in *Modern Love.*

A second device derived from the Greek Anthology is the *epigram,* by which the inhabitants of Spoon River speak intimately of themselves, in microbiographies, revealing their essential lives from the vantage point of the grave. At times Masters goes directly to the Greek Anthology, as when he writes a gloss of Simonides' well-known epigram:

O passerby, tell the Lacedaemonians that we lie here obeying their orders.[2]

Displaying his abhorrence of war and suspicion of jingoistic leadership, Masters writes:

[2] J. W. Mackail, *Select Epigrams from the Greek Anthology* (London and New York, 1906), p. 150. Although Mackail's translations were done at the beginning of our century in this revised edition, and in prose, they remain, as Dudley Fitts has stated, an unequaled example of accuracy and elegance. They were a better model for Masters than the more commonly known, but dull, Loeb Library prose renditions.

## Unknown Soldiers

Stranger! Tell the people of Spoon River two things:
First that we lie here, obeying their words;
And next that had we known what was back of their words
We should not be lying here!

*—The New Spoon River*

But more often, it is not the words of any one poem from
the Greek that shine through, but rather a general attitude,
or merely an affinity of tone. When we read poems from the
Anthology, like the bitter epigram,

At sixty I, Dionysios, lie in my grave.
I was from Tarsos,
I never married and wish my father had not.[3]

we find a modern equivalent in Masters' despairing lines:

### Robert Carpenter

You were good soil, mother of me.
Mary Woolridge,
But why did you allow the poor seed of my father
to be wasted in such soil?

*—The New Spoon River*

Masters' use of the epigram also provides the essential
connections between the voices in his work: as often in the
Greek Anthology, his personages speak to or about each
other. The interrelated voices produce a series of plots that
give both volumes the unobtrusive substructure of a play for
voices, a kind of *auto sacramental* in which abstract vices and
virtues converse. Analogues to the *linked epigram* may also
be found in the *Danse Macabre, Danza de la Muerte,* and
*Totendanz* of medieval literature, in which people from
every station reveal themselves in dramatic monologues as
they encounter death.

In her sensitive introduction to the first *Spoon River
Anthology,* May Swenson notes the parallel between Dylan
Thomas's play for voices, *Under Milk Wood,* and Masters'
*Anthology.* She remarks:

[3] Willis Barnstone, *Greek Lyric Poetry,* 2d ed. (New York,
1967), p. 259.

In scope, at least, Masters was the more daring, not to say extravagant. His ghosts freely gossip about each other and themselves, as well as about the private lives of neighbors still alive in their village. Masters let them be fearless in their sex revelations, and by this he branded himself as the Kinsey of his day. Few of the ingredients of human corruption and vulnerability are missing from the dispositions of these underground witnesses, and the Anthology remains fascinating if for nothing else than to untangle the lurid web of small town scandal provocatively placed before us.[4]

The anthology as a new vehicle of expression is one of Masters' main contributions. But how well do the individual poems stand up? There can be no hedging here. Many are bad—prosaic bits of polemics riding on cliché ideas. Masters overpopulated his cemetery hill. This in some ways reflects his own total career as a writer: two remarkable books among a mass of secondary efforts. But while many poems are poor, others are powerful and original, and add to the cumulative, grave, and dramatic effect of the *Anthologies*. Poems and lines stand out. Sometimes lines convey the severe realism of an early Lowell's *Life Studies* when he asks,

> Who harbors bums and thieves,
> and gives them beer and free lunch?,

or when he writes,

> Michael Gallagher
> Forgive me, Jesus of Nazareth, for the comparison:
> But you and I stood silent for like reasons,
> You as a lamb disdaining to wrangle;
> I as a goat tied in the garbage dump of Spoon River . . .
>
> —*The New Spoon River*

In speaking of *Life Studies*, M. L. Rosenthal writes that Lowell "also received clues . . . from Masters' characters at their most disillusioned and nervously disturbed."[5] It is particularly in Masters' savage portraiture that the wrecked

---

[4]*Spoon River Anthology*, by Edgar Lee Masters, with a New Introduction by May Swenson (New York; Collier Books, 1965), p. 12.

[5] M. L. Rosenthal, *The New Poets* (New York, 1967), p. 61.

figures of *Spoon River* resemble Lowell's snapshots of Czar Lepke or the "Mad Negro Soldier Confined at Munich."

Some of Masters' polemical poems read like an earlier Andrei Voznesensky *engagé*, but marred by hackneyed catalogues of abstract qualities, which remove the poem from the concrete image and reduce it to a set of conceptual syllogisms. But when the poet *engagé* is effective, we hear that rare voice in the arts: a voice of social conscience with the passion and aesthetic shape of individual confession. It is then that social and personal–existential elements merge. One famous example of this fusion is e. e. cummings' flashy poem on the conscientious objector, "I Sing of Olaf"— strong and violent enough but ultimately graced and softened by cummings' irony and humor. Masters' poem "Dick Sapper" is more primitive, more savage, more bitter. It is also more pertinent today:

. . .
Well, the war came on, and Ezra Fink
had written a letter to Spoon River
to buy bonds until we were broke,
And I opposed it and even opposed
The lawless and hellish draft in the name
Of Jesus of Nazareth, as I thought.
So they put me in prison for twenty years,
Where my body broke, and my spirit broke,
And where in vain I tried to be pardoned.
And I coughed and cursed to that awful moment
When the blood of my body shot from my mouth
Like a gushing hose, and I was dead.
And some of you call this a republic!
Well, some of you be damned,
And God damned!

We must go back to the Greek Anthology to find the same total bitterness and misanthropy:

After eating little and drinking less,
I suffered the pains of lingering disease.
I have lived long and now am dead. I say:
a curse on you all![6]
—Anonymous

[6] Barnstone, *Greek Lyric Poetry*, p. 257.

Masters' *Anthology* is peopled with despairing figures, like
Sophie Wassner. Sophie's wisdom lies in her awaking to the
meaninglessness of her life:

> . . .
> I was dowered with personal beauty,
> With grace and brilliancy of mind;
> Yet I married the wrong man,
> And chose the wrong friend,
> And bought the wrong house,
> And made my home in Spoon River
> To my undoing,
> Till at forty-five I awoke to see
> That all my life was wasted,
> And nothing was left to me but to grieve
> To the day of my death!

*—The New Spoon River*

The Greeks summed up the nothingness of life without
meaning in the following epigram, which parallels Masters
in its contrast of light with darkness.

> All is laughter and dust. And all is nothing,
> since out of unreason comes all that is.[7]

*—Glykon*

In the latter part of *Spoon River Anthology* there are
some notes of light, and also of death as a deliverance. We
find poems that recall Damaskios' modest epigram:

> Zozime, you were a slave girl only in body
> and now find freedom for your body too.[8]

But *The New Spoon River* contains few moments of full
optimism. Masters' attitudes have hardened since 1915. He
uses a diction that is at once city—colloquial and visceral;
and when the poems work, they are more powerful than
equivalent poems in the first *Anthology*.

In any comparative evaluation of Masters' two *Anthologies*,
a few major lines of distinction may be drawn. Although the

[7] *Ibid.*, p. 245.
[8] *Ibid.*, p. 241.

first *Anthology* contains a greater number of good poems,
the best poems in *The New Spoon River* are perhaps superior
to any in the first book; they are more desperate and violent,
more tragic. Both volumes have a similar crescendo of voice
drama, although the plots and subplots are more distinct in
the first volume. Both works begin with a small-town, *ubi sunt*
prologue; but the first *Anthology* terminates with two regret-
table sections, the *The Spooniad* and the *Epilogue*. One
theme common to both *Anthologies* is the disturbing invasion
by urban and industrial values. Village life is shaken, its
homilies exposed and denounced. Yet the city, with its cheap
funeral parlors, automats, ruthless bankers, and its "weeds
of races," is seen as both a liberation and a new disaster.
Masters was fascinated and repelled by mechanical civilization and the conspiracies of urban power interests. In *The
New Spoon River*, the intrusion of city life is more pro-
nounced. Marx, the sign painter, puts slogans on the wall:

> When Spoon River became a ganglion
> For the monster brain in Chicago
> These were the signs I painted, which showed
> Who rules America.

His signs,

> Chew Floss's gum and keep your teeth;
> Twenty-five dollars for a complete funeral . . . ,

have the cheap fanfare of billboard diction pieced into Hart
Crane's early *Bridge* poems:

> *. . . and past*   Stick your patent name on a signboard
> *the din and*   brother—all over—going west—young man
> *slogans of*   Tintex—Japalac—Certain-teed Overalls ads . . .
> *the year—*
> —"The River"

Masters took the word coined in the city, stamped out by
machines, pasted on walls and billboards, and slipped it
permanently into the diction of American poetry.

Through the sequences of related epigrams, a cranky,
honest voice prevails. Its modernity is striking. Masters sets
down common speech, as a playwright might record what

he overhears from the monologues of a drunk or a madman. He incorporates these lines in his poetry—like found poems—and by an unpredictable skill miraculously turns the common into brief Goyaesque portraits. He astounds us with reality. When his poems are effective, they are half body-punch, half meditation.

His figures speaking from the grave are more direct than they could have been in life. In a suicide poem, he captures that second of transition from this side of existence

### Evalena Fayner

Now only to get away. Quick! An open window.
Hey! On the sill. The awful leap!
Thump! Globes of circling lights,
Star showers! Blackness!

*—The New Spoon River*

"Star showers! Blackness!" The Greeks said, "All is laughter and dust." Masters remained to the end an inconsolable pessimist: not because of facile skepticism, but because he wanted more; he was profoundly wounded because life ran out on him, and, like an arrested adolescent, he was forced to live with his dreams. Masters is one of the darkest, most tragic poets America has produced: he could never wake, from wasted dreams, to anything more than the garrulous ghost-talk of unending sleep.

Willis Barnstone

Amherst, Massachusetts
1967

# The Valley of Stillness

*Where is the hope of happiness,*
*And where the faith in friends,*
*And where the loyalty in love,*
*And where the peace of plenty that never came,*
*And where the sorrows that were of life,*
*And the struggles that ceased not,*
*And the laughter that turned to tears,*
*And the tears scorched dry in the dearth of days?—*
*All, all are vanished in the Stillness of the Valley*
*Beyond The Hill!*

. . .

*Their happiness was sown in shallow soil,*
*And its root withered.*
*Their faith was as water,*
*And the star of wormwood fell in it.*
*Their loyalty was broken as a pitcher,*
*And as the empty cup of a beggar*
*It was held to the day of palsied hands.*
*And their peace came and departed as summer.*
*And their struggles, and their laughter*
*Passed from silence to sound and to silence again:*
*Voices of the night which cry and cry not.—*
*All, all are vanished and taken away*
*Into the Valley of Stillness*
*Beyond The Hill!*

. . .

*Victory and defeat are no more;*
*Deceit and trust are no more;*
*The gift of love is no more;*
*That which is received with gladness,*
*And that which is rejected is no more.*
*No more do they search here,*

1

Nor desire here,
Nor wound, nor heal,
Nor plan, nor build,
Nor labor, nor take in marriage,
Nor slay, nor hunt, nor lust,
Nor envy, nor covet;
Nor wonder whether to eat or fast,
Deny or affirm,
Act or refrain from acting,
Stand back or dare;
Or whether to act and regard not,
Or act and think of the gain;
Or fight for the inner truth of the soul.
They laid down these burdens of earth
At the foot of The Hill,
Beyond which is the Valley of Stillness!

. . .

Where are the pure of heart,
The givers of gladness,
The eyes that misted with pity,
The eyes that shone with truth,
The hands whose touch was life,
The lips that withheld not kisses,
And spoke no evil;
The lovers, the singers, the dreamers,
Who knew the secrets of sacred gardens,
And told them in words that die not?
They were as white winged eagles
Rising from the sea to heaven,
Even as waves that turn to eagles,
And fade into the light of the sky.
All, all are vanished into the Valley of Stillness
Beyond The Hill!

. . .

Where is the Abyss that shall be closed,
And the Keys of Death that shall be broken?
Where is the Ark of the Covenant,
And the Bowls of Gold with the prayers of the saints,
And the sea of glass mingled with fire?
Where is the search for righteousness,

2

*And the visions of pure rivers of water,*
*And the city that has no need of the sun,*
*And the life everlasting?*
*Lo! the hope thereof is with us*
*In the village beside The Hill,*
*Which is this side the Valley of Stillness!*

## Captain Robinson

If the tune "Spoon River," played by the nameless fiddler,
Heard by me as a youth in the evenings of fifty-seven,
By the cabin door on the banks of the little stream,
May under the genius hands of Percy Grainger
Become a symphony utterable to the baton
Of great conductors, and only thus, in brasses,
Viols, violins, flutes, and strings of the harp,
The boom of the drum, the thunder tubes of the organ—
If this may be, may not my dream of the sixties
Flower to a drama of song, a great Republic?
Till the smoke of the cabin, the smell of honey and corn,
And days of labor, and evenings of neighborly talk,
And nights of peaceful sleep under friendly stars,
And courage, and singing nerves, and honest hope,
And freedom for men to live as men, and laughter,
And all sweet things that ripple the tune of the fiddler,
Become a symphony rich and deep as the sea!

## Marx the Sign Painter

When Spoon River became a ganglion
For the monster brain Chicago
These were the signs I painted, which showed
What ruled America:
Vote for Patrick Kelly and save taxes;
I am for men, and this is the cigar;
This generation shall not see death,
Hear Pastor Valentine;
Eat Healthina and live;
Chew Floss's gum and keep your teeth;
Twenty-five dollars for a complete funeral;
Insure your life;
Three per cent. for your money;
Come to the automat.
And if there is any evidence
Of a civilization better,
I'd like to see the signs.

# McDowell Young

Whether it was the wiring up
Of the sixteen candle power of Spoon River
With the Pharos of Chicago;
And the canning works controlled by the trust;
Or whether the weeds of races kept
Obscure by the blossom American,
And all at once shot forth—
Somehow in going over my plates
I saw that the village names were changed;
And instead of Churchill, Spears and Rutledge,
It was Schoenwald and Stefanik,
And Berkowitz and Garnadello,
Aud Rubel, Swire and Lukasewski,
And Destinn, Geisler and De Rose.
And then I said with a sinking heart,
Good-by Republic, old dear!

# Edith Bell

Miss Middleton opened her door a little
To get the secrets of people passing.
And Mrs. Kessler, the washer woman,
Read the cartouches on pillows and napkins
But I with receivers clamped to my ears,
In a back room over Trainor's Drug Store
Learned all the secrets of Spoon River
While plugging wires and snapping switches:
Who was happy, and who was wretched;
And who was in love, and who was out of it;
And who was to wed, or have a baby;
And who was meeting who in Chicago;
And who was kind and who was cruel;
And who was a friend, and who a foe;
And who was plotting, hiding, lying,
Making money, or losing the game.
And I say the commandment not to judge
Went out with the telephone!

## Thomas Degges

For long years just my helper and I
With our spades, and myself to open the gate.
And outside those terrified to enter,
However wretched in homes, however homeless,
Or broken, poor, sick, weary or hopeless,
Yet dreading to enter the peacefulest home of all.
Later an office here by the gate,
Noisy with typists, stenographers,
Adding machines, the hum of dictation,
The opening of books and safes,
And cabinets of steel;
Going to lunch and coming from lunch
Yet as of old those terrified to enter
The peacefulest home of all.
And as of old the sovereignty of the spade,
Ruling now the typewriter and the card cabinet!

## Bruno Bean

With the advent of the automobile
I turned my stable into a garage,
And worked as a chauffeur now and then.
But I saw no change in the game of men,
And nothing gained by the swifter wheels:
A mounted copper chased the buggy;
And a motor cycle chases the auto;
You speed to hide, there are other speeders;
A punctured tire is a winded horse;
And instead of hay and corn and stalls,
There's rubber and gas and oil and padlocks;
And if there isn't a whip to wind
The lines around, there are levers and brakes,
And groves by the river, though farther away,
As quickly reached in a car!

# Willis Beggs

Did I reach the pinnacle of success,
Friends of Spoon River?
Did thrift, industry, courage, honesty
Used for the increase of the canning works
Become other than thrift, industry, courage, honesty
As applied to the canning works?
Are the mechanics of civilization
Civilization itself?
Or are they tools with which factories may be built,
Or Parthenons?
I fashioned my own prison, friends of Spoon River;
I put walls between myself and a full life,
Between myself and happiness,
Except the happiness of work.
And all the while I could look out of a window
Upon an America perishing for life,
Never to be attained
By thrift, industry and courage
Dedicated to the canning works!

## Ezra Fink

Raised in the faith of Elliott Hawkins of old,
Making my way as a hand on the farm,
Then teaching school, then becoming a lawyer;
Entering politics, cultivating the good people,
A church member too—
(Observe my lecture on the fall of Athens,
Due to her immoral and un-Christian life.)
Elected a judge at last of the City Court.
Then lifted up to a law partnership in Chicago,
Fighting the eight hour day,
And consolidating industries.
On and on, up and up—always busy.
Abstemious, the husband of one wife—nothing else!
Called at last to the presidency of the Trust.
Master now of tens of thousands of workers,
And hundreds of millions of gold.
Taking over the little canning works of Spoon River;
Building a church in Spoon River,
Head of Spoon River's library board,
And supervising the selection of its books.
Building myself a great tomb in Spoon River,
For which these words are the inscription:
"Blessed are the dead which die in the Lord."

## Henry Breckenridge

I used to clerk for Justice Arnett,
And write the entries in his docket,
Which fell on his head and caused his death,
Shaken off the shelf by the heave of the air,
When the gasoline tanks in the canning works
Blew up and burned "Butch" Weldy.
A change came over the life of Spoon River:
They set up The City Court, and abolished
The Justice Courts, and elected me clerk.
And instead of a justice fat and friendly,
The choice of a little group of our own,
We had these judges in black silk robes
Controlled by Ezra Fink from afar.
And instead of fun and wit and speeches,
And juries that laughed and cried by turns,
(Eloquence then was an honored gift),
The litigants entered like swine for slaughter,
And were shot from the court room premium hams;
With juries sitting like wooden Indians,
Signing the verdict the court directed.
And if a judge fell off the bench,
Or a docket bowled him out of his job,
It was due to the breath of Ezra Fink,
Whispering in New York, as it were,
Into a radio station!

## Michael Gallagher

My name a catch word
For the use of Editor Whedon, the prohibitionist;
For Editor Wood, the tool of favored business;
For Editor Lindbloom the eunuch slicker:
Who harbors bums and thieves,
And gives them beer and free lunch?
Mike Gallagher!
Who bails the harlots and crooks?
Mike Gallagher!
Who carries the ward for the red lights,
For the card men, the racers and dancers?
Mike Gallagher!
But who never answered any of you a word?
Mike Gallagher!
Thousands who knew me knew that you lied;
No one who knew you, knew you otherwise
Than as great institutions of Malice, Egotism, Hypocrisy,
And Falsehood.
Forgive me, Jesus of Nazareth, for the comparison:
But you and I stood silent for like reasons,
You as a lamb disdaining to wrangle;
I as a goat tied in the garbage dump of Spoon River,
Eyeing the festering stuff which the scribes of the Press
Piled for flies and infection to all the town.
But who entered the kingdom of heaven before these
  scavengers?
I, Mike Gallagher!
Who said so?
Jesus of Nazareth!

# Jay Hawkins

Jay walking! Reading the head lines! Struck down
By a fliver and killed while reading
About the man-girl slayer!
For years haunting the news stands,
Waiting for the latest paper from Chicago,
Cursed with the newspaper habit:
Snuffing the powder of monstrous news
Heralding shame, and hate and murder:
What dive was raided, what rum was seized;
Who was indicted, and who was lynched;
Who got the rope at the end of the trial;
What governor, officer was accused
Of bribery, graft or peculation.
Whose picture appeared divorced or caught—
(Were they never noble, did they never achieve,
And so have their pictures printed?)
All about hating, hunting, fighting,
Lying, stealing, lusting, wasting,
Who had been killed, and who had been hanged.
And I ask if life is full of beauty,
And full of nobility and creating,
Why don't they write about it?

# Jeremiah Howell

In old Spoon River we rode our horses
Hunting ducks by the lake or river;
Now they are chasing the anise bag
Over the hills and down the hollows.
We used to walk and we used to work,
Now it's golf at the country club,
And polo ponies instead of racing.
This was a place of simple delights:
We read old books, and talked of evenings,
And rode to the country in our buggies.
Now it's the magazine and the movie,
And flivers as thick as summer flies.
The hired girl took care of the children;
To-day the governess! In order that madam
May get her name in *The Daily Ledger*,
And head a committee of dramatics!
O silken swine, with a million dollars,
Why the blue ribbon, why the prize,
For jowls that swell at the country club?
Men gorge geese for Strasburg paté.
And don't the gods make a nation's eyes
Stand out with fatness against the time
Of the slaughter and Feast of Fate?

# Ibbetson the Plumber

I failed as a painter of meadows and hills
About Spoon River:
For they hated art, and believed in work;
And hated beauty and treasured use;
And they left a soul in pain alone,
But hunted a man who was happy.
And the end of it was they starved me out.
So I set to work to drain Spoon River
Of all its deadly refuse,
With pipes and sewers and porcelain tubs
And the boon of running water:
But, oh, Spoon River, where is the plumber
To make you clean of ignorance,
And cruelty, and the money lust,
That colors its yellow bacterial plots
With pulpit spewed morality?
And who can mend the sewers of hate
That keep you sick, Spoon River?

# Lulu Kay

I made my shorthand notes so plain
That any Pitman writer can read them.
Here is the truth: when business needed
The house and lot of Daisy Fraser,
Then Daisy Fraser had to move.
What good to set up elsewhere? Listen:
The equal rights of men and women,
And their intimate association,
Made Daisy a useless functionary
In the changing life of Spoon River!

## Howard Lamson

Ice cannot shiver in the cold,
Nor stones shrink from the lapping flame.
Eyes that are sealed, no more have tears;
Ears that are stopped hear nothing ill;
Hearts turned to silt are strange to pain;
Tongues that are dumb report no loss;
Hands stiffened, well may idle be;
No sigh is from a breathless breast.
Beauty may fade, but closed eyes see not;
Sorrow may wail, but stopped ears hear not;
Work is, but folded hands need work not;
Nothing to say is for dumb tongues.
The rolling earth rolls on and on
With trees and stones and winding streams—
My dream is what the hill-side dreams!

# Olaf Lindbloom

Here am I, an editor of the new Spoon River,
Son of an emigrant to America
For liberty and opportunity—
Always feeling my way.
Publishing Girondist doctrines of the largest acceptance,
Thereby increasing my circulation;
Then selling advertising space
On the basis of my circulation.
Advocating tepid reforms,
Like just taxation—dodging my own taxes the while.
Fighting crime waves, and criminals,
But myself engaged in land thefts,
And forging history through the writing and selling of news
By a monopoly of telegraphs.
Against a free press, except mine and my kind.
A leader of the unions of money,
A foe of the unions of labor,
Causing them to be jailed and killed.
An advocate of slick laws.
Against the saloons and the gambling house,
But friend to the private cellar, the back room of the bank.
Unknown and elusive,
Insatiable as to money,
A Christian gentleman,
An editor of the new era!

# Mayor Marston

Every mayor before me, far back as memory ran
Had been denounced as a demagogue dreamer,
Or else as a thief or a crook—
Yet I took the place with a hope,
Intending to beautify, give the people their money's wort
Make big offenders toe the mark.
As of old *The Ledger* was trying to sell
Its land for a park, but I balked that.
Then I whacked the noses of monstrous swine
Away from the trough. What happened? Well
The crime wave broke—in *The Ledger*'s pages!
What hold-ups, gamblers, lawless booze,
And places of vice!
The churches began to chatter,
And the courts took a hand against me.
They blackened my name, and the name of the town—
They killed me to get their way.
And this is the bandit game, my friends,
Of what is called democracy!

# George Masterman

Stranger! I saw electric lights come to Spoon River
Without a protest.
But when I inaugurated kerosene lamps for the streets
You opposed me,
Saying it was an interference with the divine plan,
Which had ordained darkness for the night;
And that lighted streets would cause people
To remain out late,
Producing rheumatism and immorality;
And that thieves would be emboldened,
And horses frightened.
You were wrong about all these things,
But you never learn anything.
You are still obstructing
The lighting of the streets of thought and life
With your ideas about the divine plan,
And your ideas about morals!

## Rev. John Onstott

Did he not say, Lo I am with you always,
Even unto the end of the earth?
Did he not say, I will send unto you the Comforter?
Were the promises fulfilled?
What say you of the passion of Spinoza
If it be not of his spirit?
And of the art of Raphael
If it be not inspired by him?
What say you of the cathedrals
San Marco and the Madeline,
Saint Peter's and the Duomo?
Were they not built to honor him,
And are they not manifestations of his essence?
What say you of Beethoven and Handel and Bach,
And the star gathering song of Dante,
And the tenderness of Shakespeare penetrating the hard
    simplicity,
The external lines and surfaces of Æschylus?
What say you of Voltaire,
Scourging the evil that he scourged?
And of Luther creating a new era in his name?
What of me, a frail embodiment of his power,
Seeking to effect his secrets in this little corner?
And teaching that when all materials and bodies,
Eras, states of life, economies, and fields of action
Of this age and ages to come, have been exhausted
And made worthless and brittle, mere dead dust
By the power of his flame,
Some evolution of him will further sublimate life?

## Rhoda Pitkin

Seth Compton died, and by that alone
We banished Volney, Haeckel and Darwin;
And then came Carnegie, who gave us a building,
And Ezra Fink, who gave us the books.
And think! I was Ezra's boyhood teacher,
And helped to make him the man he became.
How proud I was to be the librarian!
For due to Ezra's power and care
He chose the committee that bought the books,
And thus we started to mould our children
On history, religion and pure fiction,
And make them patriots, law abiders,
The builders of homes, and true Americans!
For what you feed them determines people:
Meat for muscle, and truth for brains.
And who can tell what youth will arise,
To be the president, run the country,
And keep it prosperous, safe and pure,
Out of the books which Ezra Fink
Gave and controlled for Spoon River?

## Louis Raguse

Here lies the body of Louis Raguse,
The criminal lawyer,
Whose bulging brow packed with debates
Bumped the window pane of Spoon River's outlook
With restless rebellions.
He was a lecturer of facetious paradox,
And the author of many pamphlets
Which reported his chameleon opinions,
As he veered from Jesus to Paine, and then to Nietzsche.
He was a pessimist, but only by word of mouth;
For he lived utility for notoriety and money.
He was a cautious rebel,
Having many habitations in the neighborhood of Mammon.
His ethical skin was thick
From handling and reaching for fees.
He resented death with atheism,
Hating it as the work of the Christian God.
He was the idol of the back-hall, being plain,
Unclean, pathetic and weary looking like Jesus.
All the while his safety box was full of bonds.
He understood the criminal mind;
He fathomed the hate of the poor.
But he loathed charity: let the poor unite against the rich.
He was neither a master man nor a martyr.
He was a sophisticated Caliban.
He longed for fame, he had notoriety.
He has ceased to buzz at the window.
He was a criminal lawyer!

## Emerson Rush

Here am I, after many wanderings over the earth,
Back home, honoring and honored by Spoon River!
How I remembered the forty dollars I saved
From picking blackberries,
And the day of my departure for New York
To start a magazine.
But I took more than forty dollars with me—
Also the knowledge of what the people of America
Wanted in a magazine;
And the idea that the people of America
Are just the people of Spoon River.
And at last my magazine sold in millions.
Never helped by Ezra Fink—no need,
We were equals and friends!
"The spider taketh hold with her hands,
And is in kings' palaces!"

# Dick Sapper

The ordinance of Spoon River permitted
The preaching of Jesus on the streets,
By Salvationists and Fundamentalists.
So I went to the square one day with the Bible
And began to read: "Woe unto you lawyers,
Who build the sepulchers of the prophets."
And being known as a Socialist
They put me in jail for talking socialism
On the public square.
Well, the war came on, and Ezra Fink
Had written a letter to Spoon River
To buy war bonds until we were broke,
And I opposed it and even opposed
The lawless and hellish draft in the name
Of Jesus of Nazareth, as I thought.
So they put me in prison for twenty years,
Where my body broke, and my spirit broke,
And where in vain I tried to be pardoned.
And I coughed and cursed to that awful moment
When the blood of my body shot from my mouth
Like a gushing hose, and I was dead.
And some of you call this a republic!
Well, some of you be damned,
And God damned!

## Unknown Soldiers

Stranger! Tell the people of Spoon River two things:
First that we lie here, obeying their words;
And next that had we known what was back of their words
We should not be lying here!

## Nast Wheeland

Editor Whedon used to carry
At the head of his editorial column
For motto: "The home against the saloon."
And all of his life he stirred them up,
And wrung their noses to make them fight.
They quarreled to be sure, and seemed at war,
But really at heart they were always friends.
For when the battle was over, the field
Was swept, it seemed, of the vile saloon,
And the home was victor. But what had happened?
The home had captured the vile saloon,
And taken him in to nurse his wounds,
And had him petted from cellar to garret,
Where home made beer and home made wine,
And whisky distilled from corn and potatoes
Were served as freely, as once they were served
In Burchard's roaring grog shop!

# Yet Sing Low

Yee Bow was killed by the son of Rev. Wiley;
And they wound his pig tail around his head,
And buried him near Chase Henry.
No laundry for me,
But the Golden Pheasant,
Where I served steak as well as chop suey.
And I wore their clothes and cut my cue,
And read the magazines and the dailies,
No longer a Chinese heathen.
But did I forget my City of Flowers?
No! For I lighted my pipe and dreamed:
And the water spouts on Bindle's Block
Were twisted dolphins on temple roofs;
The ash barrels in the alley became
Buddhas in bronze by an ivied wall;
The water tower seemed like a pagoda
At Ta-Li Fu, and the lilac bushes
Spread into courtyards full of blossoms.
Ding! went the register, boom went the drum,
As the Salvation Army passed and shouted
The blood of the Lamb . . . but I heard the bells
And gongs of Buddha, on high, far away,
Where a poppy moon hangs over the hills
As yellow as moth wings, under a sky
As white as the shrines or the glistening streams
In the Valley of Fragrant Springs!

## Roland Aborowicz

Life of me what were you but a dream,
In which myself was not known, but all too well
Known at the last, seen of myself as they saw me
Who stared and wondered I saw not myself as I was?
What was I but an earth born, earth bound form
Fighting to free myself from the shapeless earth,
Become all flesh and spirit in head and brow,
Chest and arms, and feet that were loosed or winged?
Never to rise from the soil, and run and dance!
But always to struggle, and push with desperate hands
The earth that was almost flesh, then turned to earth
As my hands mired down in the soil with which they strove:
I was an artist soul who never was free,
Never arose from the malice of matter that pulls
Against the soul that would fly!

## Zorbaugh Zwenen

Nineteen-eighteen, second year of the war!
I stood with the multitude, viewing the procession
Of soldiers, cavalry, bands and fluttering flags,
Lifting my hat to the flag in procession,
Not to some little flags stuck on a cannon.
Grove Trumbull, a German sympathizer,
And playing the hypocrite to hide it,
Rushed over to me with, "Lift your hat."
And struck me!
And all in a moment I was lynched!
You do not need laws in times of war
To suppress free speech—
The mob will do it better!

## Ella Snook, the Postmistress

I could read every character in Spoon River
By the way they treated the matter of letters.
There were those who never came to the post office,
Unless I met them on the street and told them there was
    a letter for them.
They didn't seem to care whether any one ever wrote them
    or not.
Then there were those who haunted the post office for letters,
And rarely got a letter.
There are two kinds of people:
Those who are sufficient to themselves,
And those who depend on the outside world,
And haunt the post office!

# Lilah Wood

When *The Ledger* became a daily,
With Mr. Wood arrived at sixty,
He celebrated his name at the head
Of the editorial column
As editor and owner
By marrying me, who was just nineteen.
And it all seemed happy enough at first,
And full of peace and prestige,
Until I knew of the game of life.
For when I began to rub the lameness
Out of his back, and mix his toddies,
And lie by his side when he was tired,
He whispered the secrets of his strength,
And the secrets of his weakness.
There were two giants, so he said,
The paper mill and the advertisers;
Perhaps there were four, and one was the bank,
And one the telegraph service.
And they almost owned him, and quite controlled him.
And there we sat in an equal fate—
For didn't he own me?

## Euripides Alexopoulos

I had a vision at last:
A divine youth was playing a harp near Trainor's Drug Store.
They listened, passed, conferred on the matter.
They returned and told him to work or get out of town.
He began then to carry coal and sell newspapers,
Playing his harp in the evenings.
The neighbors complained:
He was leading people to idleness, dreams.
He went on playing, emerged to the streets again.
Some tore at him, others hooted him, some praised him;
But he was in need of money, always money.
He put his harp by to work for money . . . no money for
    harping!
He took forth his harp again.
The strings were loose, it had to be tuned.
He tuned it and played better than ever.
In the midst of this his money was taken from him.
Shadows had come over him, he was no longer young.
His children were half grown, making voracious demands.
Should he play the harp or work for the children?
Every one said, work for the children.
They must feed and be educated,
And what is this harping after all?
They caught him then and put him to work.
His beard grew long and gray, his eyes were haggard,
He was bent, his hands were thick and dull.
He could neither work now nor play the harp.
Suddenly as he was sitting on a bench in the park
He shed his rags, as the sun sheds clouds.
He rose to the spire of the church,
Stood on one foot,
And spit on the town—
It was Apollo!

## Chalkley Cameron

If the Declaration of Independence
Is the soul of the Constitution,
Why can you never get a court
To test ordinances and laws
By the inalienable right of the pursuit of happiness?
Here was I, a young lawyer with my first case,
Attacking an ordinance of Spoon River
Which forbade the ballet,
And arguing that it was void because it interfered
With the pursuit of happiness.
Well, the judges smiled at me,
And the crowd hooted me,
And I didn't have a friend but my client,
And some of the ballet girls.
And I faded out for shame.

## Erastus Wilson

It was day-break,
And they ordered the colored regiment over the top.
I wasn't scared, but in a daze.
And I clambered out of the trench and ran,
Thinking of nothing but where the bullet
Would get me right through the heart, or where;
And whether I'd have a second to know,
Or say a prayer or something.
Thud! And my breast was turned to stone. . . .
"Good mornin', Jesus!"

## *Hosea Chambers*

You can be sure, ye living ones,
That every lie you speak or live,
However small,
Is like a brick or a board out of line or plumb
In the house of your life;
And every lie that you speak or live
Will call for another lie in line or in plumb with that lie,
Till your house will lean and stand awry,
Visible against gray clouds,
And against moonless midnights;
Visible even when the north star is hidden!

## Mrs. Gard Waful

My grandmother kept house and made the garden,
And span and cooked and raised ten children.
My mother headed a house that was kept
By servants, and raised three children.
But I knew the art of running a club,
And how to select a receiving committee,
And how to speak at a luncheon given
For visiting celebrities.
And there is my daughter Marylin,
Known to the press at ten years old,
And fated to be a noted actress—
See to it, new Spoon River!

## Diamandi Viktoria

My people came to the U.S.A.
To live in a land of liberty.
But I grew up in the U.S.A.
In metropolized Spoon River.
And I saw that the thing is money, money,
And the gift of the gab for liberty.
So I was elected county treasurer,
And cleaned up quite a roll.
You can fool all the people part of the time—
And that is enough.

## Mary Howe

Friends! This spot where I lie
Was chosen by Rev. Juda Tittle
In the belief that it was here
That my ruin was accomplished by Lucius Atherton.
And this is an accepted story in Spoon River.
Alas! how false!
I never saw Lucius Atherton but once in my life;
And then he was on the stage of Bindle's Opera House,
Where he was trying to recite Hamlet's soliloquy,
And in the midst of it had his utterance choked
By the falling down of his upper false teeth!

## Yank Sword

You get so used to saying a thing
Like: "All ready," "Over they go,"
"Just a moment," "Head of the Army,"
"I object," or "Next"—
That's it's really yourself at the end of life,
And how can you tell when out of your head,
And dying whether you say it,
Or a voice is saying it to you?
And I who had barbered all of them,
From A. D. Blood to Lucius Atherton,
And told them stories, and laughed at theirs,
And shaved them in their coffins,
Thought I was working in my shop
Dyeing the hair of Henry Bennett,
When a voice said, "Next"—and even yet
I think the voice was mine!

## Bertha Dube

Wishing to renew the friendship of school days—
Nothing else—
I phoned Paine Howard, who asked me to dinner.
I had not seen him for fifteen years.
Was it my widow's weeds, or changed face
That made him look so strange,
And look even stranger when he saw
That I was a little deaf?
What made him order so many cocktails?
And how did we get to that room?
But when the bell boy left
I flung myself face down on the bed,
And cried and cried, and prayed and prayed:
"Save me, precious Saviour, from this terrible temptation!"
Suddenly he shook me by the shoulder and said:
"God has answered your prayer, Bertha,
"Besides, I need another drink."—
What an escape!

## Socrates Chrysovergis

Do you remember that the wounded foot of Philoctetes
Stank so that no one could endure his presence?
Even so the soul with an incurable sorrow must withdraw!

## Rev. Freemont Deadman

I tried them with sermons:
"Temptation," "Choosing a Character,"
"The Unmarried Mother," All no good!
I gave them theology, God-head demonstrations,
The sacraments and scheme of salvation—
Empty pews and the church in debt!
I gave them a travelogue: Yellowstone Park with Views—
Quite a crowd: the movie was closed for repairs that night.
Then the Rev. Althoff Bilge and I
Joined hands to save the churches:
We got up suppers at the Pekin Tea Gardens.
Allowed the young to dance square dances
To saxophones, served ginger-ale!
It wouldn't do, for it wasn't real;
We couldn't compete with the children of darkness.
I quit at last and began to lecture—
You see I needed money!

## Lewis Fay

No justice without hate for steam;
No law without revenge;
No charity without partial love;
No belief without closed eyes;
No forgiveness without recompense;
No service without some gain;
No labor without a lure;
No sacrifice without a heaven.
Sun and shadow, reality and image,
And myself worn down with hollow words,
Activities, hopes, and dreams,
Dodging devils and seeking the gods!

## Gordon Halicka

I sat and looked at the river
Riffled and stirred by the wind;
But I saw that the depths of the river
Were moved by the under stream.
Two visions came out of the river,
And the wind and the under stream:
And one was the face of a woman,
And one was the shaking of reeds.
For the water riffled and dimpled,
And ran into smiles and frowns.
And the reeds were whipping each other,
And torn by the under stream.
And even an oak by the river
Had fallen into the stream!

## Watson Stelinger

If any garage had hired as chauffeurs
Reckless boys or murderous hoodlums,
Who had harried the streets like battle chariots
Armed with scythes . . . would you have stood it?
If aeroplanes in the hands of imps
Had skimmed the streets, and ruined the roofs,
While their secret owners laughed at terror,
Or called it fate when life was taken,
Would you have suffered this, Spoon River,
Or gone for the torch, the ax, the rope?
And yet these editors, Wood and Lindbloom,
Turned their engines of presses and paper
Over to ignorant writers, who wrecked
The names and peace of helpless people;
And you hired for critics of art and books
Venomous women and envious men,
Who soiled the truth and tortured beauty,
To please themselves and you!

## Barton Halsey

Beware of weak friends,
And common paths:—
In the days of your decline
You will take to them
As the only solace,
And the only support of your failing strength.

# Silas Jennings

A democrat!
A believer in the rule of the people!
An agitator for laws to be made by the people
To control greed, injustice;
Then an agitator for laws to be made by the people
To control tastes, thoughts, expressions.
A democrat become a despot,
Denying the equal rights of souls before the law of the soul,
And violating that inner democracy
Through which souls are equal as to beliefs,
Tastes, expressions, joys, wisdoms, visions of life.
A democrat turned mobocrat and fanatic;
A watch dog seized with rabies;
A Judas betraying spiritual freedom,
By persuading the eleven to vote it down.
A false prophet giving dumbness for speech,
Blindness for eyes,
Paralysis for health,
And seven devils for one!
Carve for me a calf with the head of a donkey,
And wings of an eagle,
And feet of a dragon,
And eyed with one eye like a cormorant!

## Nicholas Koslowski

Of my many sculptures keep at least the one
Of the Illini in the throes of hunger,
On the heights, but starving.
In that bitter winter of the war
You could give coal and food
To the fathers and mothers of soldiers,
All your vision strained to the glory of war—
But no coal, no food for me,
Who by sculpture alone could make you freer,
And democracy wider and more beautiful
Than all the soldiers who ever lived!

## Levy Silver

Why did I sell you plated silver,
Rhine stones and synthetic rubies?
Why did I sell you gold filled cases?
The question at stake is why did you buy?
I couldn't sell them as real and prosper.
But you could buy and pretend them real,
As part of your game of fooling each other
With fake morality, hollow customs,
And laws compounded of spurious stuff.
The goods I sold matched something in you:
For some of your souls were only plated;
And some of you put yourself together
To imitate virtues clear and precious:
And some of you were mostly brass
Under a film of gold!

## *Thomas MacCracken*

New commandments I give to you, Spoon River,
Out of the wisdom of living:
Thou shalt make graven images of all beautiful things;
Thou shalt take the name of God in vain,
For by unanswered prayers shall you be lifted up;
Thou shalt labor every day in the week,
Even as thy heart rests not;
Thou shalt give life;
Thou shalt love the woman who gives her love to thee,
Or else thou shalt not accept her love;
Thou shalt help to multiply the goods of the community;
Thou shalt tell the truth about thy neighbor,
And about thy enemy.
Thou shalt be free, joyous, tolerant, active.
Thou shalt trust death,
Having trusted and rejoiced in birth!

## Judge Donald Shuman

It gave me a lesson in resignation
To see that nothing of ceremony
Makes anything of death.
I went with a wreath for the grave of Judge Loeffler;
The sexton sent me to the office,
And a brisk stenographer took the wreath,
And said the judge was still in a vault with others,
She didn't know the number.
Then I remembered the shocking report of his death,
And how they laid him out—not the end.
His friends then viewed him—not the end.
He lay in the court house in state—not the end.
He was taken to church, and they sang and preached—
Still not the end.
He was prayed over at the vault—not the end.
He is still in the vault—not the end.
He is yet to be buried. And will that end it?
All this to prolong an episode
That ended when he died.

## Catherine Ogg

"Tombstone" Johnson, head of the school board,
Ashamed that he sprang from an egg,
And a wriggling sperm,
But proud that man was created from dust,
Though dust is dirtier than eggs,
Ousted me from my place in the school
For showing a picture to the pupils
Of a child emerging from an egg shell,
And telling them all the beauty and wonder
Of evolution that makes a mind
Out of an egg and sperm.
So I retired and struggled along,
And starved a little, and brooded much
To the end of the farce!

# Ambassador Saul

My father was Jake Saul, the butcher,
Who got into the trust, and moved to Chicago,
And became a millionaire,
And died and left me millions,
And I married millions.
We had a place in society—but it was equivocal—
("He's the son of old Jake Saul," they said)—
So she whispered to me to be appointed
Ambassador to Holland—
(I spoke Dutch, you know, as well as English.)
So the millions came in handy now,
And I was appointed, and went abroad.
And we saw ourselves in the London papers
Side by side with the pictures of kings—
I was Ambassador Saul!

## Frank Treadway

Here lies Frank Treadway
The lost hope of his father William Treadway.
He gave his soul to the Prince of Peace,
Who sent the sword of discord into our home,
Before that a place of tranquil happiness,
And set him at variance with his mother,
His brothers, his sisters,
And his father, who carves these sorrowing words!

## Joseph Walsh

We who withhold our names,
Silent voices of the annals of Spoon River,
Have erected this stone as a tribute
To the life of Joseph Walsh
Whose strength was shattered by great misfortune,
But who continued to the end in wisdom and nobility,
Even as a vessel of gold remains gold
After it is broken!

### William Alston

Friends, could you imagine of me
A deed like this:
Would I have spread a field
Of artificial clover,
And tempted my bees forth with lamps
Only to let them starve?
Children of men! Swarming races!
The field of clover is as real
As the hunger that seeks it.

## Henry Yewdall

I was one of the reporters of *The Ledger*,
Gradually drilled down from reporting events as I saw them
To reporting them as they wanted to print them.
If they had only challenged the truth of my report!
They didn't.
They only said that what I reported wouldn't please;
It didn't represent what should be;
It didn't represent what never could be.
It had to be better or worse than the fact—
It had to sell the paper!

## I. Start

How often, Friends of Spoon River,
Did the Rev. Abner Peet denounce the disbelief
And stubbornness of the human race,
Using the text wherewith to do it
Which is found in St. Luke:
"If they hear not Moses and the prophets,
Neither will they be persuaded
Though one rose from the dead."
Is that true? No, my friends, it is utterly false!
Let me out of here and I will convert the whole world!

## Hicks Boscawen

You who are still in life,
And torn with the problem of choices,
Take your way.
But you will find it as well
To lie slushed in the sands of satiety
As to break upon the rocks of discontent,
And defeated desire.
Is there a middle course?
Anchor near the shore and drowse!

## Henry Zoll the Miller

Have you ever noticed the mill pond in the dog days?
How it breeds wriggling life,
And seethes and crackles with poisonous froth,
Then lies as still as a snake gone blind?
And how can the mill pond know itself
When its water has caked to scum and worms?
And how can it know the world or the sky
When it has no mirror with which to see them?
But the river above the bend is wise:
Its waters are swift and cold and clear,
Always changing and always fresh,
And full of ripples and swirls and waves,
That image a thousand stars by night,
And a thousand phases of sun and clouds,
By a changing movie of forest and hills!
And down in its healthful depths the pickerel
Chase each other like silver shadows;
And the swift game fish swim up the stream.
Well, this is the soul of a man, my friend:
You brood at first, then froth with regret,
Then cake with hatred, and sink to dullness;
Or else you struggle and keep on the move,
Forget and solve and learn and emerge,
Full of sparkle and stars.
And down in your depths there's flashing laughter,
Swimming against the current!

## Lucille Lusk

There is nothing makes me sorrier for men
Than their emotions about virginity:
How they prize it, how they rave for its loss,
And revenge its loss.
Lucius Atherton took my virginity.
And wasn't I as well off for losing as he for winning?
I married another man afterwards,
And lived happily enough.
And I could name you twenty women in this graveyard,
Spinisters of the church, patricians, grand ladies,
Who secretly and without the consent of the county clerk
Gave up their virginity,
The same as they shed their baby teeth,
And not many years afterward.

## *Jacob Braham*

In your mortal days did you not see
That man is linked to every living thing
By kindred ties of physical substance and form,
And by ties of physical need and function?
And that the thing called life
Is the same, whether in plant or beast or man?
And when you saw that man's body was not alone
In the world of created beings,
And that man's life was not alone
In the world of living beings,
Did it not give you the hint that man's soul is not alone,
But is companioned and sustained
By genera of spirits,
And by hierarchies of gods,
Bound together by the same spiritual blood,
And rising by creative evolutions
To kinship with God Himself?

## Madison Matlock

Passer-by! Not only did I lose health and fortune
In the search and vision which were mine in life,
But I lost your esteem as well for losing my heart's desire.
I was not like the veterans of wars,
Admired for my disabled body and mind,
And pointed to as a hero of great battles.
No, I was smiled at as one who had failed and lost,
Having staked everything on a vision.
No pension for me! No reverence for a creeping strength!
Was my life a failure then? Did I lose?
I succeeded, I won!
Having seen visions, and dreamed dreams
Beyond anything you can imagine
Who give medals, and reward with donatives!

## Ernst Fidazko

I fled from Prague to escape the law,
And came to Spoon River.
But after I married the sister of August Fortune,
And he took me into business with him,
My story leaked out and it crippled me.
His name was good and mine was bad.
And she I married suspected me,
And August handled me with tongs,
And all the people talked and talked.
Well, I talked back to protect myself
Against them all, August and her.
And envy drove me to secret slander,
And the business suffered as I plotted.
And my own ruin engulfed their ruin.
All bad. But wasn't it fate?

## August Fortune

Ernst Fidazko was born in Prague,
And I in Spoon River.
And he was himself, and I was myself,
As unrelated as Iser and Big Creek
Then like a torpedo, blind as fate,
Shot in the waters to wreck and ruin,
He crossed the sea and came to Spoon River,
Not knowing me, nor the town,
Nor my sister whom he married at last.
And thus he thrust what he was
Of treachery, lying and greed
Into the good I had made for myself,
Like a floating mine in a queenly ship.
And soiled my name and wrecked my fortune.
Where is the wisdom to keep those out of your life,
Who are wandering mines or torpedoes?

# Harvey Williams

I was as good as she at the start;
But afterward she became the milliner,
And looked like a walking hollyhock
With her parasol and tony swagger.
While I shoed horses to make a showing,
Really supported by her;
And mowed the lawn, and tended the garden,
And sprinkled the flowers, and ran her errands,
To earn and keep her love.
At last her frequent trips to Chicago
Buying goods, as she said, together
With certain questions from Benjamin Pantier,
And Jonathan Somers, and such:
"Well, Harvey, where's your wife?"
Got into my brain and made me think.
So while I was shoeing that wicked mule,
I stood for a moment and stared at his hoofs,
And said to myself in an idle way:
"She loves me, loves me not."
Well, quick as lightning I fell like a feather
Into an ocean of ink.

## Rita Matlock Gruenberg

Grandmother! You who sang to green valleys,
And passed to a sweet repose at ninety-six,
Here is your little Rita at last
Grown old, grown forty-nine;
Here stretched on your grave under the winter stars,
With the rustle of oak leaves over my head;
Piecing together strength for the act,
Last thoughts, memories, asking how I am here!
After wandering afar, over the world,
Life in cities, marriages, motherhood—
(They all married, and I am homeless, alone.)
Grandmother! I have not lacked in strength,
Nor will, nor courage. No! I have honored you
With a life that used these gifts of your blood.
But I was caught in trap after trap in the years.
At last the cruelest trap of all.
Then I fought the bars, pried open the door,
Crawled through—but it suddenly sprang shut,
And tore me to death as I used your courage
To free myself!
Grandmother! Fold me to your breast again.
Make me earth with you for the blossoms of spring—
Grandmother!

## Teresa Pashkowsky

How came this Japanese poppy
To bloom alone, far afield in a middle meadow,
With grasses and yellow buttercups around it,
Lifting its scarlet splendor, bright as a flame,
Like a ruddy moon, like a torch in the earth bound hands
Of buried Persephone, high over flowering weeds?—
A wind blew the seed from a lovely garden,
Over the soft warm waters at night, when the stars
Fringed down or lifted lashes of drowsy light
For the soothing heat of September.
But whence were you, Teresa Pashkowsky,
Here amid drug-stores, movies, squabble and alleys,
Rising to song, and the soul of Lucia, Thaïs,
And fame in the world?

## *Bertrand Hume*

To recall and revision blue skies;
To imagine the summer's clouds;
To remember mountains and wooded slopes,
And the blue of October water;
To face the shark gray spray of the sea;
To listen in dreams to voices singing,
Voices departed, but never forgotten;
To feel the kisses of vanished lips,
And see the eyes of rapture,
And hear the whispers of sacred midnights. . . .
To live over the richness of life,
Never fully lived;
To see it all, as from a window that looks
Upon a garden of flowers and distant hills,
From which your broken body is barred. . . .
O life! O unutterable beauty,
To leave you, knowing that you were never loved enough,
Wishing to live you all over
With all the soul's wise will!

## Lincoln Reeth

Oh, little town by the river,
Little town of little hopes,
I am your son, in spite of myself,
Though not related to you.
But here is my fate; the tablet of bronze
On the house I was born in there in Spoon River
Brings pilgrims from over the country;
While my very grave by Emerson's,
Since I lived and died in Boston,
Evokes from the passer-by such things
As: "Lincoln Reeth! Lincoln Reeth—
Who in the devil was he?"

## Claud Antle

All are sent into the thicket of life,
Some to hunt and survive, some to be hunted to death.
What was it that gave them the scent of me,
Made them pursue, and fortuned Fate and Nature
In a league against me, all along the way?
First as a boy, teased and fought by schoolmates;
Bitten by dogs, nearly drowned, sick to death
From eating toadstools; always a broken arm,
Or the kick of a horse, or a frozen ear.
Later betrayed and robbed in business.
Beauty of person, gifts availed me nothing.
I was a deer compelled to live with the hounds!

# The Tombs of the Governors

### Forgotten Governors

We are the forgotten rulers.
We have left no story
Of our great friends who maneuvered us into office,
And stood behind the throne after we were in.
Some of us waved the bloody shirt and were elected;
Some of us were elected
Because our fathers were able wavers of the bloody shirt.
All of us were creatures of interests,
Little beliefs, empty programs,
Deceiving promises.
Living for nothing, we left nothing.
Our memories died with the deaths
Of our patrons and protégés,
And those who attended the New Years' parties
At the executive mansion.

### Abraham Lincoln Pugsley

I worked my way through business college,
And received the degree of M.A.—
Master of Accounts.
I taught school and studied law at night.
I became a judge of election, then precinct captain,
Then a committeeman with a string of delegates,
Then master of a district, all the while practicing law.
I forced my nomination for state's attorney,
Helped by the reform newspapers, and was elected.
Instead of taking bribes from saloon keepers and gamblers,
As my predecessor did,
I prosecuted them, and multiplied the prosecutions,
Forcing them to plead guilty—and I grabbed the fines,
And became rich on fines.
I was powerful now, and forced my nomination for governor.

I entered the executive office empty headed, but befriended
By the powers that fight saloon keepers and gamblers,
And the labor unions.
Traditions, liberties, philosophies
Were nothing to me.
I even tried for a third term,
But I saw the storm coming, and slipped into the cellar
Of private life.
Around me are the graves of the soldiers
Killed in a strike that I crushed—
I was a governor of the state!

## Elliott Hawkins Hammond

No pioneer, nor the son of one—
A lawyer's son, and a college man,
A real sophisticate from the start,
A twentieth century product.
I took my cue from Lambert Hutchins
Who sold his vote in the legislature
To the railroad that wanted the water front
There in Chicago—but I was a "Packard"
Where he was only a democrat wagon:
I headed a legislative committee
Commissioned to decide the titles
To lands submerged on the water front.
And thus instead of having a purse
Slipped to me for a favoring vote,
I edged along, and edged along,
And pecked away at the giant Theft,
Until it was almost ready to fall.
Well, who could shore it up but me?
And I shored it up for contributions,
Ten thousand here, ten thousand there.
Then the war came on! And I plunged in,
And risked my life for the sacred cause
Of the world made safe for democracy.
When I came back a grateful people
Elected me their governor!

## Walter Ehle

Passer-by! I was an idealist,
A dumb singer of the ideal;
And I warn you: both commandments and ideals
Are only external mottoes
By which life is not meant to be lived,
And which Life in anger at last
Tears from the walls and throws away.
Discard them first yourself,
And live by the unwritten law of the hour.
Here was I with love in my heart;
Then staring the motto "Love" long after
She began to dispraise me, and wound me,
Her vanity and self-sufficiency fed by my love.
Then she fled to Europe, leaving me in loneliness,
And to solve the fate she made for me
As best I could.
With what a rattle of glass and splintered moulding
The motto "Love" fell down from the wall
Of that hotel room in New York
When I saw her in the arms of the purser
Of an Atlantic liner!

## Edward Hill

Where there is love of the art, there the love of man is;
And where the love of man is, there is love of the art.
How deeper is the creative virtue of these words
Than the words: where a man's treasure is there is his heart
    also!
I was the son of the good and tireless physician,
Myself a painter of the fields
For the delight of Spoon River!

# The Seese Lot

### Ferdinand Seese

I was the youngest of twelve children,
Born of aging Jacob and Susannah Seese,
Myself of feeble body and weak will.
A demon of self-destruction had me from the first
To wreck my health and wreck my life,
And punish myself with terms in jail,
And to ease myself and kill myself with dope.
These were the fowls of the air which devoured me—
Why did the sower sow me by the wayside?

### Charles Seese

I was the eleventh son of twelve children
Born of aging Jacob and Susannah Seese,
A good seed no less, but needing earth and rain
To mature me.
I strove to succeed in Spoon River,
And to establish my mind and my life.
Somehow the hearts of this people
Were turned against me like flint,
And my roots withered.
Why did the sower sow me among stony places?

### William Seese

I was the third son of twelve children
Born of Jacob and Susannah Seese.
Honor and wealth seemed mine.
But I did not see what was rooted around me
In the spring of life, before the weeds sprout,
And the unleaved bushes stand unrevealed,
All of which grew as I grew.

I knew the way of the blossom, and there was space to
    grow in
As it seemed at first.
But there was my nature, and there was my father
Forcing me into a business, and into a marriage
With the daughter of his partner.
And many children taxed my strength;
And I strove for the money to rear them right;
And the weeds of sorrow sprouted around me
In giant cares, and thick disasters,
Until my strength was choked—
Why did the sower sow me among the thorns?

### Robert Seese

I was the seventh son of twelve children
Born of Jacob and Susannah Seese,
Bequeathed a sound body and a sound mind,
With will to strive and hope to win,
And guarding the prize of life.
The hearts of this people turned to me
As a crop of vetch makes soil for the corn;
And I started where my father left off,
And made the business greater than ever,
Warned by the fate of my brother William
I had three children instead of ten;
And I had an eye to dodge disaster,
For God was good to me who sowed me
In ground that was good. I did the rest
And brought forth an hundred fold.

# Hofflund the Cobbler

Henry Bennett's were white and veined;
And Daisy Fraser's rough and ruddy;
And Elliott Hawkins' breathed with lungs;
And Abner Peet's were small as a lady's;
And Flossie Cabanis' thick and stubby.
And each one had a taste of his own
To hide a fault or stress a beauty.
Petit the Poet loved thick soles;
And Mrs. Williams loved bronze leather;
And Margaret Slack a shoe that was loose;
And Lucius Atherton high-heeled boots;
And Jefferson Howard heavy brogans;
And Pennewit the razor toe.
But who do you think—(I'm telling secrets)
Had a foot like the god Apollo?
It was no other than Garrison Standard—
And he had a face like Marat!

## Gabriel Quilici

When I was a boy I heard the story
Of Ida Frickey and Harry McNeely,
And how she tricked him with a pillow
Under her waist, and got some money.
But what is money compared to the loss
Of vision, a spirit self-contained?
And what is gold to a planet decoyed
Out of its orbit in hope of realms,
Higher, freer, more ecstatic,
Only to be released of law
To drift and die in pathless darkness,
Exhausted of will, and the light of life?
Always the sirens come to the poets,
They wait on the rocks for singers to pass.
The life that sings is life to their lips;
They hate the song, for the poet is free
Of all they can do as long as he sings.
Gorgeous butterflies! lured by color;
Golden bees! after honey of thought,
Beware the sun-dew, water lily,
Beware the pitcher plant and cob-web.
Rifle the flower of innocent petals,
And store its sweet in song!

# Thomas Paine Howard

Son of the liberal Jefferson Howard,
Born as well with the joy of living,
I hated the church which fought my father
Through Rev. Peet and Rev. Wiley;
I hated it too for Flossie Cabanis,
Who joined "East Lynne" and fled the village,
And could not return for the wagging of tongues.
And so I started to fight with logic,
Emerson founded on David Hume,
And science out of Spencer, Darwin.
I threw it all over at last, in disgust,
For business, money, and started a movie,
And gave Spoon River the weekly events,
Mountains, waterfalls, and jungles,
As well as "Shylock" and "Robin Hood,"
And cells in the making, and embryos.
Well, what do you think? They flocked to me,
Deserted the hymns and the dreary sermons—
And so I wreck the churches!

# Henry Rabeneau

To be gay, free, to be a liver;
To see through the cant of service;
To hoot effectively the uplifter;
To know that life is a jest;
And man a germ amid bread and roofs;
To walk like a giant, laughing and roaring,
Kicking off the ropes of the dwarfs,
Breaking the chains of the New Jerusalemites.
To smile at all philosophies and religions,
As the mind wanderings of starving wits.
To be a fat and lusty weed,
Flaunting insolent leaves—
Then to have the dwarfs get you,
And cover you with their ideas of dishonor,
Until infinite disgust rots you,
And you wither and lisp and break,
Frost bitten and dusted over.
That was I, fellow citizens,
Until in the hour of death
One moment of myself, gay and free
And insolent, returned in a laugh!

## George Kramer

Long years ago there was Roy Butler
By Mrs. Bandle tricked and convicted.
Then in my time there was Rube Smiley
Held for a baby that wasn't his—
(I happened to be the father myself.)
Well, don't they vote, yet get supported;
And bewitch the mob that makes the laws;
And make the morals of the country;
And mould the children to suit themselves;
And own their own, and run what is ours;
And kill if they wish, and go scot free
Because of amorous judges and juries?
And there was my wife who got an increase
Of alimony behind my back,
Then jailed me because I couldn't pay.
Don't talk to me of woman's rights,
Let's hear of the wrongs of men!

## Heine La Salle

Oh, you theologians and preachers and sectarians,
And makers of rituals and creeds,
You have missed the story of Jesus,
And left it to us, the artists, children of sorrow to know it.
For the Iliad is nothing but the story of Achilles' wrath.
And the Odyssey nothing but the story of the wanderings of
    Ulysses—
But this story of Jesus is the forecast and symbol,
The epitome and epic
Of every soul, chiefly of every genius soul.
First the humble birth; then the youth of twelve,
Like Mozart conferring with the masters.
The vision of destiny then, the disappearance and preparation.
The return, a master, and the raptured words of youth.
By their side the doubt of father and mother and brethren,
And the village that knew his origin.
Then persecution, because society fears
Always the genius soul.
And that turns the sweet song sour, turns love to hate.
The betrayer among your own! Always the betrayer!
Your own sleep while you watch—the task is yours.
The cup! Terrified that it must be, wondering,
Praying that it may pass.
Darkness of the soul in the midnight of doubt,
And death.
Then Wonder, the maker of myths;
And the Intercessor, posthumous-fame,
And adoration, a thing of rote.

## Rocco Papini

Was Caesar killed for being a despot,
Or because he could rule with thought?
Have bards and wise men been destroyed
Because they wore fine linen and purple,
Or because their thought would win the world,
And rule the world?
Was I hooted at,
Was I hobbled and wounded,
Who was never a mayor, nor even an alderman,
For power usurped, or a sceptre filched?
Or was it because I almost won
The people of Spoon River
To the plan of a park, and public music,
And the art of dancing?
Very well! And did I fear you?
No, for you couldn't kill the soul!
And Caesar and I walk over the earth,
And glide through walls and bolted doors,
And walk with you as you go to Emmaus,
And burn your hearts and win your souls
In spite of nails and daggers.

## Eveleigh Loos

At this moment that you are standing by my grave
Stars are taking new positions,
The sun spouts great flames,
The earth has just reached the sign of Sagittarius.
In the sea cruel eyes turn, hungry mouths open.
In Africa a great gorilla is just shuffling through the jungle.
And in South America an anaconda has slipped heavily
From a tree to the ground.
A Mahometan has begun to pray in Egypt;
And a cannibal in the South Seas is hacking the limbs
Of a fellow being before cooking them.
In Paris chancellors are plotting in a room.
There are many partings and re-unions at this moment,
And promises made and broken.
A great man has just died in Bombay;
And Mrs. Seese has given birth to another child,
Here in Spoon River.
I am dead, and you are standing by my grave—
All at this moment!

# Thomas Wentworth Arlington

After you have married and begotten a son,
And the son grows up, and you see in his eyes,
And see in his ways, the crookedness,
Always suspected, and almost proven
In the father of her you married:
There it is at last! Etched clear, definite, beyond dispute.
This was my fate who married the daughter
Of Thomas Rhodes, the hypocrite banker.
And what could I do but stand aghast
Like a hen that hatches a snake?

## Edward Redington

Which is the better: the joy of growing perfect apples,
Or the joy of raising apples to trade for better apples?
In life I was the doer of good deeds,
Moved by the doctrines of the church.
I forgave in order that I might be forgiven;
I was merciful, believing that I should obtain mercy;
I gave, hoping to have the measure heaped in return.
With what treasure was my soul enriched?
With the treasure of expected rewards!
Then as I was not forgiven,
And as I did not obtain mercy,
And as I was not given unto,
The fruit of my labor was wasted,
And soured in the bins of my soul,
Being unpaid for by those for whom it was raised.
And I say unto you, act for the Self,
In order that the Self, in spite of others,
May be enriched by forgiveness for its own sake;
And mercy for its own sake;
And generosity, courage, steadfastness,
Absence of envy and pride,
For their own sakes and for the Self!

## Ezekias Painter

Considering your heredity, O my Savior,
And that your ancestor Roboam was a bad man,
And begat Abia, a bad son;
And that the said Abia, a bad father,
Begat Asa, a good son;
And that Asa, a good father,
Begat Josophat, a good son;
And that Josophat begat Joram,
Of whom nothing is known;
Who in turn begat Ozias, of whom nothing is known;
And on down, until your father Joseph was born,
Of whom nothing is known,
Except that it took an angel from heaven
To keep him from divorcing your mother Mary—
Seeing all this, and that my father was a drunkard,
And I a leader in the church, a man of substance,
I must conclude from your case and my own
That neither piety nor impiety
Is hereditary—
Which makes me fear for my son!

# The Unknown

Have you ever become conscious of the thrush in the
    cherry tree
Only when he ceased to sing?
And then gone out to find him with broken wings
Lying in the syringa bushes?
Have you ever seen a man in the streets
Walking slowly with head down;
And afterwards learned his fate
When he became articulate on a bed of pain?
Have you known a man clothed with the light of Fame,
And bugles of clearest silver blown for him,
To sink into silence, followed by the tramp
Of the feet of collected hate?
Have you known a man to fall at last
Incurably wounded by love?
What fate was mine?
I have hidden my name
To hide my story!

## Martin Venable

Did you ever destroy a bird's nest,
So there was not a vestige of it left in the tree?
Then have you watched the bird when it returned,
And flew about and about the place where the nest had been,
Wondering what had become of the nest,
Or wondering if this be the tree of the nest?
It was even so with me and Spoon River:
I returned to find the old town
And found it not;
And drifted about wondering
If Spoon River had ever been my home,
And if so what had become of Spoon River!

## *Mark Paas*

Tranced as a youth with the plangent strophes of Milton,
The singing flame of Shelley, and O you songs
Starring the tragic clouds of Shakespeare's vision—
I said to myself, the hand of death could not still you,
Death could not blot and vulgarize your souls
With darkness forever, and nothingness and silence.
But oh those last days in April, days of my life the last,
To hear the robin spired against the sunset,
Or the thrush, with the sweet of the meadows wafted to me
There by my window, sick and torn with thought:
So many springs! So many thrushes and robins,
Gone like the poets I loved—and into silence?
The song of the robin sharpened my darkest doubt!

## Herbert Nitze

Did you ever think what a mess it would be
If all the people ever born, even within four thousand years,
Were still on the earth?
Moses with same old lingo;
Aristotle arguing his ideas, too old to change;
(Don't we have a taste of this in distinguished octogenar-
    ians?)
Kings! walking the automat, trying to pass old pennies;
Crusaders! chattering of dead centuries in the drug store;
And Ponce de Leon, still looking for youth,
Bothering us for bail, pinched under the Blue Sky law;
And Roger Bacon trying to make gold;
Not to take the Cro-Magnons,
Who would talk art, demand to get in exhibits,
All this! And the young and middle aged
Compelled to adjust with men of a thousand or more,
Diet, ideas, money arrangements, amusements, places to live.
O Death! waster of spent leaves,
Fall gardener, clearing the ground for spring,
You are wise, you are Nature!

## *Jabez Arnold*

You living ones
Do you know what you are,
And what is being done with you?
You are leaves on the stem of life,
And the stem of life and the root of life
Are using you to extract from the Infinite
What shall return to the Infinite—
Involution and evolution forever!
This is the secret, manifested materially before your eyes
In the leaves of the trees,
Which extract from the sun and the air
Sweets and colors,
And hand them on to the stems
And the roots of the tree,
Until the leaves have given all,
And nothing remains of them but ashes,
And the flush of exhaustion,
From ultimate sacrifice!

## Clara Viall

Do not sow the seed,
Keep it in the granary;
Tell it to transform its desire to become a field of gold
To the spontaneous heat that warms the granary—
(And burns it at last, perhaps.)
Let the acorn lie between rocks;
Tell it to lick the cold shale
With the tongue of a white and yellow sprout,
And to be satisfied.
Tell men and women to repress, to sublimate
Passion to service, life to duty,
Until sacrificial smiles warm the neighborhood.
Go on with your sadistic ideals,
Whose soldiers break the bones of penitents
Upon the cross of defeated life.
But carve for me a granary afire,
From which a swallow is swiftly flying
To smokeless skies!

## Frank Blatt

Here I lie, rotted down from two hundred pounds of flesh
To less than a pound of mud.
After eating four hundred steers,
And two thousand bushels of corn,
And ten thousand loaves of bread,
And drinking five thousand gallons of whisky.
What for? To give me strength to blat,
So that I could buy beef and bread and whisky,
And blat!

## Mrs. Frank Blatt

Where would my mother and my sisters have been buried,
Not to speak of myself,
If I had not married Frank Blatt. . . .
I the stenographer, fat and a little old?
And at what board would my mother and sisters
Have fed,
If I had not captured him and he had not taken them in,
There to that household of the full larder,
And the mortgaged roof?
Here we are then, lying around Frank Blatt,
We the Blatts, and my mother and sisters the Wallups!
Passing from corn and beef
To the bread which whoso eats, lives forever!

## Mistral Visyana

This is my sorrow,
O my beautiful flowers:
That I did not sow you
In better soil.

## Amy Bardwell

He entered the room of my life,
Where I sat balanced in joy and pain,
And smote the air of my peace with his story
Of his wretchedness with his wife.
I loved my husband, but had forgotten;
And I fled with this man to find new life,
Fooled by the light of love!
But what is love? Is it only to say
You love, and yield your lips to the man?
Or is love living, till every mirror,
Tapestry, lamp and shelf of books
Has taken your souls and become your souls?
And so when I fled, the table cloth
Entangled me, dragged the cups and pitcher
From the Feast of Life to wreck on the floor.
Could I go back to a room of ruins?
New cups and pitchers cannot be won.
And so I sat at a lonely window,
And watched him pass, and smile on his wife,
Whom he returned to, leaving me
To mend my broken goblets!

## Linford Newman

Triumphant amid the many realms of this life—
Realms of greed, of hate and of strife—
There is the realm of the wise and the just,
Lying above us as a glory within a glory
To which we can rise for fellowship
As a plant stands up from the breaking hands of the wind
To the air and dew of heaven!
Realm of vision! Realm of truth! Realm of love!
Open to us in hours of doubt and pain
When black hands claw us from the pit.
This is the good faith of the perseverance of the saints,
Raised to the higher heaven of Beauty!
O, great ones who are dead, yet live;
And O, ye living ones over the earth
Who shall never die,
Leave ajar the gates of your paradise of light
That we may commune with you;
And rise from the commonalty of little living
To the fellowship of wisdom and dreams!

## Felix Beam

Is the restlessness of life concerned with bread and honors,
Or is it caused by bread and honors?
Was my going to and fro in the earth,
Days of doubt, nights of waking,
Due to anxiety
About bread and honors?
Friends deceive not yourselves:
The intense center of the soul's maelstrom
Whirls forever, and becomes a vacuum of wonder
And searching:
"What is Thy name?"

## Melton the Tailor

I built up the shoulders of Henry Bennett
To win him the love of Rosy Jenny;
And tightened the trousers of Lucius Atherton
To trim the fat of four and forty.
And I fashioned cut-aways, Prince Alberts,
And modest grays for quiet gentlemen,
And opera coats for dashing devils
When the town became Chicago's suburb.
But even my best work had to be altered:—
For you dress them at last like laying leaves
One by one on a bed of pansies:—
And so you slit the coat down the back,
And the trousers too, and lay them on—
And thus they're tailored for heaven!

## Maud Shook

If I had lived in the early days
When there was no telephone,
Nor even a telegraph,
And all the trains were slow,
And the mails came once a week,
I might have believed he wrote me a letter,
And that the letter was lost.
But just as the chances of not hearing
Are lessened by mails and telegraphs,
Suspicion in you increases.
So the soul goes down as machines go up,
Or else you must build your soul all over
To the new and intricate calculus.
And I thought at the last I should have written
Another letter. For, O Spoon River,
Belief in the soul you love is better
Than any pride of self!

## Jerry Benson

Did any of your newspapers, Spoon River,
Or your claquers for the sacredness of law,
Or your moralists or preachers
Open your mouths against our bloody bondage.
And the oppression which strangled us,
And the wages and the hours which robbed us
Of the gift of life, and darkened our homes,
And killed our wives and children?
But the moment a few men were blown up,
At the canning works,
You dumped, like a thousand of brick,
All the moralities and laws upon us;
You turned the steam into the monstrous crusher
Of the sovereign state.
Yet not one of you would have dared
To have counted lives with me!

# Marjorie Hungerford

Such waste of granite and fruitful land!
Put a tablet of bronze on this house of mine.
Say that I loved it, made it a place of beauty;
Say that I dreamed here, often stood at the window
In rapturous springs, hearing the robin at dawn.
Say that my friends were feasted here and were happy.
Say that I waited here for the one great friend.
Say that he came and knew my house and loved it,
And kissed the door because my hand had touched it,
And kissed the step because it had known my feet.
Say that life at last to me was heaven.
But as the Fall draws Summer, and Summer Spring
Into the year that melts in the light of Time,
Say he was drawn away, and I walked the halls,
And stood by the window, naming the distant stars.
Then say that I closed the house, and made it a Temple
To Memory, a tomb of departed Beauty.
O world! O time! If fire or decay destroy
This house of mine, keep for a little the tablet,
Keep it, though it pass to ignorant hands or mocking—
I have done my part by the Beauty I loved and lost!

## Marshall Carpenter

Remember not your Creator
In the days of your youth,
But remember your Youth in the days of your creator:
Remember how you felt, aspired, loved;
Remember your visions and faiths,
And the beliefs in yourself and others.
Remember whom you chose,
And whom you rejected, and why.
Remember how you looked to others,
And for what you were taken by others.
Remember your house and its trees,
And the village.
Remember the subtle ways of air
Which blew aside intangible curtains,
And showed you what you could not report.
Thus hold to yourself and grow
To yourself as an oak,
Turning never to an alder bush,
Or sand grass!

## Didymus Hupp

If God is all and in all, as I opine,
Then God is also in quinine;
Also in whisky and in wine;
In flesh of steers and flesh of swine;
Sometimes evil, sometimes benign;
Honey and milk and iodine.
Whatever you do or drink or design
You get too much of Him in fine;
For a man is only a branch of the vine—
I did and here at last recline.

# Henry Cogdal

Bring from a Big Creek a huge boulder,
Put it at the head of me,
And bolt upon it a tablet of bronze
With these words:
Here was buried the body of Henry Cogdal,
A private who fell in the war for Wisdom,
And Beauty and Truth.
He strove to be a guide to the creative spirit,
And to uphold the singers and tellers of stories,
Who keep the vision of a nation
Upon the clear realities of life.
At the height of his power and work
He lost his place and means of support
Through a rich manufacturer who bought the newspaper,
And began to popularize it,
And to lower its criticisms
To the level of advertisers and optimists:—
There will come a time when crimes against culture
Will be punished the same as murder!

## Reason Robb

You would have thought that she was ruined,
You would never have thought that I was ruined,
By her wrong of me with Lucius Atherton
Caught, divorced and written up
In Editor Whedon's paper!
Well, while I was living calm and strong
What does she do but go away
Quiet, smiling and wise,
To return a linguist, teaching the drama,
Lithographed over the whole of Spoon River,
And entertained by the Wash McNeelys,
And all the prominent people!
And what were my virtues, pride and character?
And where was my triumph in life?
My soul was steel, but what of that?
Her soul was a force electrolytic
That shattered my soul to crystals!

## Sarah Dewitt

Because I believed God brought him to me,
And because I believed him gifted of God
With honor, truth and love of the right,
I believed in God and worshipped God.
Then when I found he was just a thief,
And full of treasons and perjuries,
All for money and worldly pride,
The wreck of him was the wreck of God;
And so I fainted amid the ruins
Of plaster and sticks, and sat in the stillness
That followed the fallen bust of God.
Friends, it is folly to prison God
In any house that is built with hands,
In man or woman, or passionate hopes,
Or the love of Truth, or the Rock of Ages.
For all will change, deceive or crumble,
As soon as you think you have prisoned God
For God is Proteus, and flies like magic
From earth to heaven, from hope to hope.
You never can catch Him, and this is the reason:
The game of the soul is never to find,
The game of the soul is to follow!

# John Fiske Roberts

Was I an atheist? Did I put God out of the Universe?
Then did not Jesus put God out of the Universe when he said:
"For the earth bringeth forth fruit of herself."
Did the race of man ascend from primal life,
Even as a man comes from a cell?
"First the blade, then the ear,
After that the full corn in the ear."
What came over you, Spoon River,
That with the end of the Great War,
Waged for Liberty,
You began to slop all wisdom and all truth
With the deep sea slime of dead protophyta,
The scummy ignorance of the Middle Ages,
Starving me, and almost mobbing me
For my lecture on Darwin!

# Morgan Oakley

There is a time for vine leaves in the hair,
And a time for thorns on the brow,
Even as life is both ecstasy and agony,
And as Nature grows both leaves and thorns.
In youth I knew love and victory;
In age loneliness and pain.
But life is to be lived neither as leaves,
Nor as thorns, but through both.
I came to the wisdom of barren boughs,
And the desolation of unleaved thorns,
Which remembered the leaves!

## Blincoe Blight

Of what use, Spoon River, was it
That the Jesus you worship, (and in whose name
You falsely abolished the saloon from the land,)
Rung the bell of enduring truth when he said,
That what enters at the mouth goes into the belly,
And is cast into the draught;
But what proceeds from the mouth
Comes from the heart?
And since lying, and perjury,
And fraud, and sneaking and bribery,
And adulteration leading to death,
And hatred of law for its sake and its makers,
Comes from the mouths of this people,
You are blind as adders who cannot see
That you've swallowed a camel to put such things
In the hearts of men;
And strained at a gnat to forbid to them
A little wine in their bellies.
And so I cursed you going blind,
And cursed you as I died!

## Edmund Pathe

Passers by! If you have a sorrow
It is well for you if you are among friends
Who know your sorrow, and know you.
For their knowledge of you and your sorrow
Helps you to endure it.
Either they will sustain you with tenderness to bear it;
Or else they will resist your leaning it upon them,
And thereby make you see it, as it is.
But oh, what a fate was mine who lived to the time
When only a few knew me,
And no one knew, or remembered my sorrow.
That is the tragedy of the soul
In pain and alone as the darkness deepens!

# Ike Sass

Here in the Annex, but near the grave
Of Harry Wilmans who died for the honor
Of the flag in a charge through a steaming swamp
Near far away Manila;
And close as well to Captain Killion
Who died at last from wounds received
Fighting to save the Union,
Is the grave of me, who fell for the rights
Of little nations, democracy,
And the freedom of the seas!
But Harry Wilmans died for sugar;
And Captain Killion died for iron;
And as for myself I died for an empire
Of ciliated gold.
And up from the grave I send this word
To the boys in days to come:
When you hear the bugles, and hear the preachers,
And God is talked, and Death is flouted,
Don't let them fool you, for all of the noise
Is the growl of hungry guts!

# Watson Watt

Of what good was it, Spoon River,
For me to rebuild my shattered reputation
Among you, the mob, the howlers for blood,
By joining you in your shrieks for slaughter
In the Great War?
I rode into power again and prestige
Thrilling you all with my oratory,
Which belied the truth I knew,
And sickened my heart that said to me:
"I know what you are after."
Well, after the war, the great debacle,
Where was I?
Just there with you, the mob, the cannibals,
The dull Decaturs, big and little,
With my reputation as good as yours,
Accepted by you, and no better now;
Rich at the bank, but poor of soul,
For having danced and howled with you
To recover a waning prestige!

## Mary Borden

Just as he always bought green wood,
Which sizzled and dripped water
As I tried to cook with it;
So did the fire of his love
Burn my heart to tears.
After all our heartaches,
His and mine,
What was it but this:
The heart that loves you will make you weep!

## Ernest Tyron

I preached the faith of pessimism.
But do you know the secret?
'Twas love of life, and hate of death
Which ends and so dishonors life
That made me rail in bitterness,
Life is not worth the living.
But if you love a thing you fight
Even for means to keep the thing.
And if you love a thing you think
It has some use to you.
That's why, though failing at forty years,
I set to work to build again
For fear of starving in old age;
And found myself restored in fortune
Before I came to sixty.

## Leonard Failes

Why did you bury me next to Ernest Tyron
The theoretical pessimist?
For I was the real thing.
Failing in the laundry business at forty years of age
I lay down and never worked again.
What was the use?
There was no use, and I lived the idea to eighty years,
Supported by wife and children!

## Evalena Fayner

Every night for a year
Eyes suddenly opened to thrilling silence—
Then the clock struck two!
And tossing till day in the torture of memory
Of ruined happiness.
Great weariness becoming my very bones and flesh,
Past the cure of sleep, could I sleep.
Fears like hovering condor wings:
Fear of walls! Fear of crowds, of buildings.
Fear of poverty! Fear of sudden death!
Sapped, terrified by the smallest demands of the day.
Restless! Walking about and about
To get away from something! What?
To back away, to run, seek havens of distant places,
See old friends. Oh, no! Never to be endured.
Suddenly I found myself in the doctor's office,
Trembling as the door closed to with a gust and a sigh;
And from somewhere near Chopin's "Berceuse."
Now only to get away. Quick! An open window.
Hey! on the sill. The awful leap!
Thump! Globes of circling lights,
Star showers! Blackness!

## Selden Snively

Prodigal son of me! I forgave you,
When you came back from Monte Carlo
I took you in, and clothèd and fed you,
I honored you as I never had honored
My faithful Ernest who stayed at home.
But I saw at last that my forgiveness
Was due to the weakness of a kinship
Which made me favor you from the first,
And mastered me in the failing years.
For was my pardon and my honors
Good in all, and good for you?
Did they not harm the truth and your brother?
Give you a robe that belonged to Duty?
Give you a ring that belonged to Faith?
Give you a banquet, flowers and viols,
As if you had served, and dared and achieved?
How counts it with heaven which sees one goodness
Crop in a thousand ills, I wonder?
And who can be saved in just one life
Lived for forgiveness, with neither strength
Nor time to live for truth!

# Howard Snively

My father gave me my share of his estate,
And I went forth to travel and live,
And drink my fill of wine and women
In New York first, and then in Paris,
In Buenos Ayres and Monte Carlo.
I was broke at last and trailed back home
To get my father to feed and help me.
And what could I say? That I was right,
Or say I had sinned before him and heaven,
Seeing that I was ragged and hungry,
And needed food and a place to sleep?
Well, he was so glad to have me again,
For I was his pet from the day of my birth,
That he took me in and clothed and fed me,
And rejoiced that the lost was found again,
And he that was dead had come to life.
It wasn't true: I was worn with living,
Weak from excess, unnerved, diseased,
And haunted with visions of joys departed,
And stung by regret for wasted hours.
Was his forgiveness all of the story?
And was I saved for being forgiven,
Who went on living upon his bounty,
And taking thereby the share of my brother,
And being nursed and served and carried?
The very shame of it rotted my soul,
My father's goodness killed me!

## Ernest Snively

I stayed at home and helped my father
To build, enlarge, preserve his fortune.
And my brother was given his share of the money,
And went away and spent it in feasting.
Oh, yes! My father said, to console me,
That I was ever with him—why not?
I was always at home, and never intended
To leave him, even for wrong like this.
And what did it mean for my father to say
That all that he had was mine—just fooling!
My share of the money bought food for my brother;
Not mine the robe, the ring, the feast;
Not mine the honor, not mine the dancing,
Not mine the kiss, and the sickly tears.
Not mine the inheritance, Death the dicer
Took me first, and so my brother
Inherited all the money!

## Julius Brink

Most of you in Spoon River
Were critics of each other, while I was a critic of life.
And you were optimists and believers,
And I a skeptic and pessimist—yes!
But here is my faith in life and death:—
The world was many millions of years
Building itself from mist to soil.
And it took a half a million years
To turn the ape man into a Greek.
So what does it prove to show no progress
Within the time of written records?
If it takes as long to civilize man,
And make his soul stand up with his body
As it took to build the earth, what wonder?
There's time ahead to do it in—
And that was my faith to the last.

## Hughes Robinson

Follow the thinking of a woman
And you will become as crazy as she is at the last.
But the world is a woman,
And the world drives everyone crazy at last.
And in the death throe I saw the world
Eyed with two oceans, and breasted with mountains,
And just the form of a woman, I swear:
This world which stops prize fights,
And howls for war;
And calls pacifists fools,
Urging force as the great nobility,
Then crucifies workmen who use force,
And says that nothing is gained by force;
And lauds laws, and tramples laws;
And preaches love, and robs the weak—
All this insane, topsy-turvy, aimless,
Witless talking, and childishness,
This woman mind,
This insane world!

## Horace Knight

Friends! Shall your white-houses and executive mansions,
Your halls of the States and the Republic
Be occupied by the thin-lipped and the bald-headed?
By the graduates of business colleges;
The readers of subscription books;
The fanatics on economies;
The hunters of vice and crime;
The wearers of hand-me-down Prince Alberts,
And satin stuffed ties;
The interpreters of democracy as mediocrity?
Or shall the lovers, the livers,
The well sexed, the philosophers, the artists,
The viewers of life as Freedom and Beauty
Occupy your white-houses and executive mansions,
And have something to say about the Republic
Founded by Tom Paine, and Ben Franklin,
And Thomas Jefferson,
And the other bully begetters of children,
And of ideas, who knew the difference between a Rembrandt
And a chromo,
Between grape juice and Madeira;
And who knew that friendship and hospitality and happiness
Are worth all the principles and preachments in the world.

# Walter Britt

Many of you pass now on Sunday afternoons
And say: "I wish he were here."
"I'd like to talk to him to-day."
Yet for years I walked the streets of Spoon River,
And found but few who had time for a word;
Or I stayed at home, and no one called.
And when I took to my bed at last
You didn't come much, and there I lay
Lonely and longing for friendly hands.
Your time is past, fellow citizens;
Your day of grace with me is sinned away—
I have departed!

## Theodore Helpgod

Stranger! I died of hydrophobia.
I was bitten by both the upper and the under dog,
While trying to save the under dog.

## Col. John Clary

After my sacrifices in the war for the Union,
Then to live to the day of the Great War.
To lie for days in a delirium, and out of thought
And suffering to see that monster ravage the land,
With a mouth like the Grand Canyon,
Swallowing churches, swallowing colleges,
Halls, as well as tons of newspapers,
Tons of books.
To hear him snort like a storm
As he trampled Liberty into the mire,
While mouthing moralities, patriotisms,
His throat full of bells, pipe organs, the booming of cannon.
You call this a Republic,
Where happiness is hunted, delight is defeated,
Thought is throttled, speech is choked;
And where slickness, lying, thieving, hypocrisy
Are encouraged and enforced by the Great Beast?
And where Dullness, the eunuch, is enthroned
Amusing himself by swatting flies
With a scepter of lead!

## Perry Routson

Rousseau's children are now forgotten,
And he might be forgotten, too,
If he had not sent them to an orphan asylum
To free himself for the writing of books.
But oh! to be remembered
For deserting your children,
For the sake of learning the violin,
And not to learn it!

## Jonathan Somers Knapp

They found me insane
For donning the dress of a policeman,
And breaking up a dinner of Rotarians,
Who were singing "The Old Oaken Bucket,"
And talking business, and raising money
To help the Boy Scouts of America;
And playing the fool, and making fools
For a lollypop Republic!
Besides they had broken our meetings up,
Where we talked Justice and Liberty.
And I took my stand with Jesus of Nazareth,
Insane, as they said in Jerusalem,
As I was not in Spoon River!

## Albert Husband

Never since Athens, never since charity
Became the word for love, and the hydra-headed
Beast of the snake and the dove took rule in the world
Has friendship thriven between a man and a man:
The vision and flame that binds two heads and hearts
In a life of wooing the soul, and making the soul.
I had my vision, and chose my friend and loved him.
They laughed at first, and then they breathed upon me
The smell of their vile suspicions, and so I fled,
Hid my identity, wandered afar in the west.
What a bemusement, almost a soul surrender
To the blackguard mind of the town, made me reveal
My name to the nurse at last in Santa Fe?
And so to be brought where remembering swine abound,
Grunting: "Look here! The grave of that man, you know!"

## Robert Owen

Pause and consider these words, my friend:
I espoused the cause of the strikers;
And helped the defense of the rebel hearts,
Who losing, revenged themselves with bombs.
And I found myself, who was once esteemed,
And rich in money, suspected and shunned,
And fought at the bank, and broken at last,
And hounded to sickness and death at last,
All for the luring wings of a faith
In justice for men enslaved and robbed.
But what is a single soul befooled,
Compared to a nation out of its mind,
And led to a war with shouts for God,
To find it was only the Devil's mask?
A nation that for years or centuries,
Faithless, bewildered, in self-contempt
Must clear the wires of broken hopes,
And the ruined fields of liberty,
Till the Devil fools the nation again!

## Maurice Schlichter

Remembering the fate of Eugene Carman
Who confessed to his theft and threw himself
Upon the mercy of Thomas Rhodes,
I turned to the Bible for words of wisdom,
And went to the rivals of Moses Schrimski,
Successor of Thomas Rhodes, whose money
I stole for the needs of life.
I went to his rivals and told his secrets,
I went to his rivals and settled his bills
As the unjust steward did in the parable.
And when I was fired by Moses Schrimski,
I got another job in the store,
Whose owner hated Schrimski.
And I say there's no better book than the Bible
For a man in trouble like me.

## Barbara Caprile

Always two sets of eyes in the drama of two:
The eyes of the giver, the eyes of the receiver;
The eyes of the buyer, the eyes of the seller.
What a thing costs, what is the gain in the selling.
Always the loved one seeing with calm, clear sight,
That the lover walks in a vision and sees a star,
A flower, a wonder and light.
So your eyes made me, and I knew, and knew you were
    blinded
By the light that shone in your eyes because of me.
You knew me as music, sang me too,
And gave me your soul.
And what was it to me who sold and knew the gain of selling?
That I could command you, bend your will to mine,
Wear your flower of love as a trophy,
Live through your strength and sacrifice—
That was my side of these gifts of yours—
Until the Furies took me at last
Seeing your dead face emptied of all that you gave,
And all that I garnered in pride!

# The Destinn Mausoleum

### Father

The life you abhorred
From birth shall be yours,
At last be your lord.
Your purpose allures
Its enemy to you.
And all your resistance
Draws what you resist
To your heart to subdue you.

### Mother

The thing you resolve
Not to do is your deed.
Vultures revolve
Over you, they will descend
On you too weary to heed.
The face that you hated
Is the face for you fated
To take for your friend.

### Mary

Your blood is your own,
But it also belongs
To the hunger that scents it,
And never alone
Leaves you in peace
To mix it with his.
Forgetting your wrongs
You shall dream and·submit
In an opiate bliss.
You shall sit eye to eye
With the face that you purposed to fly!

## Joseph Ruhe

Urged by the wisdom
That the dead wish to speak to the living
More than the living wish to speak to the dead,
And have more to tell the living,
Than the living have to tell the dead,
I worked at my psychoradiograph
Amid the smiles of Spoon River.
And now that I am here I would tell you
The secret of love and music,
And the sorrow of hills, and vanished days
And what it is that breaks your hearts
With music and love,
While making you sing and love!

## Haeckel Schmidt

Which is the more scientific statement,
O you blind adders of Spoon River,
To say that Nature is a reckless waster of life,
And selects the strong to survive;
Or to say that God has predestined to eternal life
Those whom he has called, and those only?
Who made me sound of limb, and strong of mind,
God or Nature?
Who made Ferdinand Seese of weak body, and blind will,
God or Nature?
Who predestined him to shame and death,
And me to honor and life?
Who made you Presbyterians and me a Scientist,
Using different words for the same doctrine?

## Mortimer Covici

Search through the Bible from end to end,
You will find no verse so great as this:
"Male and female created he them!"

## Prof. John Scott

Why did you mock me, Spoon River,
For choosing the wrong son
For my love, and my hope of a great career?
Laugh at something worth a laugh:
Jesus told his disciples to go not in the way of the Gentiles,
And into the cities of Samaritans to enter not,
But rather to the lost sheep of the house of Israel.
Yet what made Christianity most beautiful,
Most imaginatively philosophical?
The Jesus forbidden genius of the goat-footed Hellas!

## Victor Brothers

Many along the way will smile to see you;
You will be dined.
Hundreds may rise to defend your name;
Some will lend you money.
But you will be blessed above the lot of millions
If in a tragic hour of falling down,
In daze and torture of soul, unable to think,
Or even to utter the word of your need, some hand
Unlocks the door of escape, when you have hurried
From door to door, finding them fastened or false.
You will be blessed if the wise, great friend appears
In that hour of your sorrow, and thinks for you,
Until you rise to strength of mind again
To think for yourself!

## Kay Rutledge

I loved hospitality and the friendly glass,
And you counted it to sin, Spoon River.
I loved a horse and a race
In the bright June days,
And you called it gambling, Spoon River.
I was the intercessor of the harlots,
And the saloon-keepers, and the ill-begotten
Who became thieves and murderers,
And you named me as a friend to vice and crime.
I spent and gave away my money,
While you became land owners and church members,
And looked down upon me, Spoon River.
I loved fiddlers, and dancers,
And the tellers of stories,
And you considered my life wasted.
I sank down into meagre means,
And helpless blindness, and loneliness—
(All the fiddlers, all my cronies gone.)—
And you saw me as the victim of unrighteousness,
And passed me by.
I died.
But did I follow you, or lead you
Into the kingdom of heaven?

## Keith Kobestich

Whatever the majority do to you,
Or those acting for the majority do to you;
However vile your injury may be,
And however calling to heaven
To rectify it and expunge it,
It is the triumph of the majority,
And the vileness of your injury wins no reversal, no victory.
Was my name vindicated?
Was my course justified,
And my wisdom proven wisdom?
When?
After I was here!
After the time had passed
When my work and course were of use in the world!

## Richard Harned

Golden bees at the heart of violets,
Heavy with starry wine of the flower,
The lizard lurks for you there in the thickets
Armed in mimesis green as the leaves.
The emerald wasp is watching the clay pots,
All day filled with your spoil of the June;
The Fab in terminal scarf of azure,
And breast bedecked in Florentine gold
Thirsts for the fruit of your toil for children
Born of her, pressed by the will to life.
And the small gray flies come trooping after
Wasps and Fabs with shark toothed jaws.
What is it all but a great devouring?
What but Nature that passes us on
From stomach to stomach, till man the spirit
Fights against spirit, devouring, devoured?
Golden bees! I died believing
All mounts up to some finest life,
All is love, and death of loving;
And if there is life that is higher than Art
It's peace that shines in God!

# Andrew Winslow

Thou shalt have no other gods before me. There must be
    other gods to have!
And what of the Trinity?
Thou shalt not take the name of the Lord in vain. What!
    No prayers?
Remember the Sabbath day. Very well, forget Constantine.
Honor thy father and thy mother! Who are my father and
    mother?
Thou shalt not kill—except in war, with the noose and
    stones.
Thou shalt not commit adultery. Very well!
The holy polygamy of Moses' day is enough.
Thou shalt not steal—save from the Philistine, by slavery
And in the game of property.
Thou shalt not bear false witness. Well, did any holy
    propagandum
Ever surpass the pillar of cloud and fire, Jehovah,
Made a cloud and a darkness to Pharaoh?
And what a trap you made of the sea!
Thou shalt not covet anything that is thy neighbor's—
But suppose it isn't his?
And how about destiny, and thunders on Mt. Sinai,
And trumpets commanding conquest?
A new commandment I give to you: love yourself.
Was I popular? Is my grave a shrine?
Look at the grass and the weeds!

## *William Seaman*

Because the Bible says, Thou shalt not kill,
They arrested me for talking on birth control.
But if the stream of life should have its way;
And if to loose it and then divert it be a crime,
Then not to loose it at all is a crime.
Why not arrest a few deliberate celibates?

## Percy Cowherd

Who is astir in the early morning?
Who lies abed?
Who wastes the milk when it sours?
Who makes cheese?
Who nosed around my barns,
And almost broke me?
Who forced me into the trust,
And thereby saved me?
What made Chicago?
The kick of a cow!
All the big milk-men
Up there now,
In a skyscraper. Gentlemen, see
I learned about everything
Just through milk.
And why compare it to human kindness?
Because it is watered or sours or contains
Germs that fatigue you? Look at that grave—
That's Roscoe Purkapile's!

## Roland Farley

Brooding light which saw not, and yet saw
What eyes saw not that needed light to see.
And thought which was all eyes, and made of life
Sound, and of inner light made thought and song.
Sight sphered in darkness, even as an urn which shuts
From the soul's candle winds of the lawless dark,
And left the soul's dreams burning in a calm
As a star hidden in the bowl of night
What one of you, Spoon River, grieved for me,
Rejoiced not in my gift for light denied;
Saw not my heaven for my sunset sea,
Nor knew my heaven and my sea were one,
One splendor and one secret sensed afar?
That light and thought and sound are one in some
Sphere where no eyes are, and no need of eyes!

## Robert Chapin

Have you stood in front of the iron bars,
And watched the lion look over your head?
He sees the palm-tree and the mate,
And the waste of the tawny desert!
Are you moved by music, or the concourse
Of melodious words?
But how are you moved except for life
That made a self of you, responding
To sounds or scenes of remembered places,
Or other spheres, perhaps?
Life is a cage! Beauty a vision
Of a freedom once enjoyed.

## Emanuel Troy

I found myself changed
As the result of everyone being changed toward me,
And so lost to me.
For what you are depends on what others are to you.
The soul is a pool of water
Which mirrors blue skies and white clouds;
Or become an undistinguished part of the meadow
Under the darkness of night.
Thus changed, and no longer known to myself,
And unable to win back the blue skies
And the white clouds of departed friends,
And thus regain myself,
I began wandering companionless and unknown,
Till my return to Spoon River,
To this spot under the tree!

## Elias Kahn

Carve for me a bunch of keys,
A ring that dangles the keys of many doors.
Passer-by! Your pockets are full of keys
Which you are no longer permitted to use.
You, too, carry the keys to many doors
Long closed to you.
You, too, have retained the keys to barred houses,
And bolted gardens.
You, too, passed from city to city,
From place to place,
Keeping or forgetting to surrender
The keys of forfeited havens!

## Righter Selden

Of what use is it to be on the point
Of coming to great wisdom through suffering,
And then to dull your vision,
And lose the wisdom
By easing your suffering
Through some anaesthetic,
Whether it be alcohol, or Christian Science?
You who do this sell all that you have,
And then fail to buy the pearl.
You who do this have left the cave of ignorance,
And the haunts of bats and sightless fish,
Only to bandage your eyes
Against the light of heaven,
And the one great star in the East!

## Wallace Hardy

You grieved when I burned your letters,
You said I had murdered your very soul
In burning your letters.
But when your child was taken from you,
What did you do but hide his coat,
And hide his little hat and shoes,
And lock away his picture,
And put out of sight whatever kept you
In thought that begged for rest?
Oh! Yes, my friend, you understood:
Life and Memory cannot live
In the house together where Love has departed,
Or Death has entered!

# *Joseph Revell*

Scale after scale of you,
Truth after truth of you peel to the core of truth,
The white, hard center of realest life.
Break the sheath and crack the shell,
Find the kernel that springs to a greener leaf,
A richer flower.
Giving gifts to purchase peace,
For acclaim, for the sake of conscience,
Or to quiet the hour of death: seed leaves,
Tear them off till you reach the core of giving,
Giving to find your soul and perfect your soul.
Love: the frayed and dusted scale of sex;
Love of family: the lioness and her cubs;
Love of your fellows: winning love for yourself—
Tear all away to the monad crystal, yourself . . .
Love that burns for the truth of love,
Love a star, not a moon!

## Gabriel Buissono

How often I left the midnight of the mine,
With its bleary lights,
For the darkness of the sky with its stars,
Until that hour that the unpropped ceiling fell,
And buried me under tons of slate,
There in the mine of the Equity Mining Company,
At the edge of Spoon River—
(Owned by the Rhodeses, Phippses and such.)—
What did it all come to?
I was killed, but I had to die anyway;
They outlived me, but died at last.
And now they are mining the infinite blackness
With phantom picks, where nothing caves,
And nothing even yields!

## Herman Sensale

How does it happen, Spoon River,
That there is free printing,
And never ending printing,
Always and everywhere,
In pamphlets, newspapers, books, periodicals,
Government reports,
As to economics, dietetics, hygiene,
And as to everything relating to the hunger of the stomach,
Whether it be food merely, or roofs,
And whatever is related to the hunger of the stomach;
While you forbid printing freely and truly,
And garble and hide and lie about what you do print
Concerning the great hunger,
To which the hunger of the stomach is only a servant:
The master hunger for mates;
And the secrets of delight and misery
Which make for unions or separations?
Would you be happy as well as prosperous?
Publish freely the economics of love,
As well as the economics of bread!

## Protopapas Demas

To run a fruit store in Spoon River.
To look at prairies at the ends of streets,
Not up at Hymettus.
To go to a little stream,
Never to see Phaleron below Olympus.
To have Turks and Persians rule you:
So called moralists, preachers and merchants.
Yet I kept still for the sake of trade,
Naturalized in Spoon River.
But I say to you, you can thin as you will
The veins of the children of Homer,
They will run red stuff compared to the veins
Of the breed of A. B. Blood!

## Ambrose Seyffert

Oh! The years we waste, and the souls we waste
In learning one simple thing—
And what it takes to teach us!
Not until after her lonely sojourn
In Buenos Ayres, leaving her children,
Who had to be left to leave her husband—
All in devotion to me.
Not until after her hopeless return
To the door of dishonor, the roof of remorse,
Did the meaning of that devotion to me
Stare like the blinded eyes of a friend
On my poor heart gifted with vision at last
To know devotion—but when it is lost.
To know devotion! Like one who knows the good of a lamp,
When the lamp is out, and he stumbles in darkness,
And falls to a fate of endless pain—
Lamenting the absent lamp forever!

# Henry Head

Do you know why I sat silent,
Always outside the circle, observing,
Scarcely speaking?
I was always thinking of my imprisonment
There in New Hampshire,
And that you might sense it.
I felt like two persons:
One the inmate yet of the prison,
Carrying the soul secrets of the prison;
The other the ghost among you,
Out of the death of the penitentiary!

## Selma Lanstrum

I was a waitress at The Fulton,
He a conductor on the electric,
When they joined Chicago with Spoon River.
And going back and forth I saw him.
He was so kind and understanding,
He treated me like a woman of worth,
And looked at me with eyes so clear,
And strode the car so straight and strong,
He was a gentleman through and through,
Who seemed to be out of place.
I lost my heart, and lost it for good.
And when he vanished I couldn't sleep.
Why, long years after, seeing his picture
In a magazine, I cried so loud
My husband shook me and accused me,
And asked "Who's that?" "Who's that?" I said—
"Knut Hamsun, a famous writer."

# Lieutenant McGrew

Carve for me an eagle crumpled amid the heights,
Shot through the breast!
For there on that day in June, winnowing rushes of mist,
And gliding through little floes of writhing spume,
Far up in the quiet sphere of sun-faded sky,
With the fields and meadows around Spoon River
Become a quilt of yellow and green,
And the river become a strip of silver foil—
My heart stops! For my engine has stopped!
Silence! She sinks like a steed that squats to leap,
And then the plunge!
The dizzy turning over and over!
Till she dives nose first with the anarch weight of steel
To the crash through the trees of Siever's woods!
And then this grave beside my father's
Who fell through bellowing darkness
Down, down in the water tower—
Carve an eagle for me!

## Louise Hedeen

Carve me a cherub! All of me head and wings,
Resting on shoulderless arms that enclosed me.
What was the heart of me? Always the head of me!
What were my longings but restless wings,
Stretched ever for flight in the wonder of waiting,
The far heard cry of a mate, or an April caprice?
Once in the midst of a spring that I searched for,
Spring that I found at the last, in a moment
Off I flew, leaving the blossoms, the vision:
Leaves of the sky between leaves of the lilac;
Skies in my wings' soft hollows, that nestled
With kisses of eyes closed down in passion.
Up then I soared searching the lips of that sky.
I broke my wing with a clinging tendril and fell,
To a covert of grass and roots, where I brooded
A beauty forsaken, nursing an endless pain!

## Emmett Burns

Passer-by! Do you know who are the slickest schemers,
And the most excellent despots?
They are those who say, this is right and this is wrong,
And who ascend the throne of what they call the right,
And then hedge the right with a law.
Is there no way to beat these shallow souls?
Follow me, passer-by:
Be young, be wise,
Be indifferent to good and evil,
And the laws they make—
Seek only the truth,
And die!

## Rollo Simone

Think you that the secret faults of your soul,
The dark sins you commit against your own nature:
Hidden hates, envies, shirkings, disbeliefs,
Fears, sloths, contempts of the struggle,
Torpors and surrenders—
That these are not known?
Think you that the terrible sins—
So terrible that you are ashamed to tell them,
And the wounded one is made too dumb to tell them—
That these committed against your friend,
Or the one you love,
Shall never be known?
Yet every one of these sins shall be known!
For daily, sin by sin;
And daily by regret of the sin,
You will be making yourself,
Until your face will be as discernible,
As if scarred by disease,
To those who have sinned as you, and know the marks!
These will tell it on you,
As a way of denying it as to themselves:
That which is done in secret
Shall be shouted from the housetops!

## Minette Henderson

I married him, entranced by his name in the world,
Not knowing his name was growing dim.
I married him though his hair was graying,
For the manhood of him, though he was poor.
Then his great friends invited us for visits,
And the witch, the charmer invited us
To her mansion house, with all its richness—
This woman, just one of his friends!
But I saw that his strong years had been given,
And the fame of his strong years to this woman;
And I saw she had taken all his gifts,
Then turned him away to marry me.
And here was I a guest in her house!
So I went to her room and wept and wept,
And wept my heart away!

## Christopher Merriam

You blamed me, friends of Spoon River,
For separating myself from my father and mother and
    brothers,
And later from my wife,
And charged me with forsaking my own flesh and blood.
But that was testing me and reproving me
Only by that lower plane of kinship
Which is seen of the eyes,
And not seen of the spirit.
Did not Jesus say, Who is my mother,
And who are my brethren?
And did he not answer that those who did his will
Were his mother and his brethren? . . .
That is to say, those who lived as he did,
And saw life as he saw it!

## Benedict Peerbolte

You may not gather grapes of thorns—
But are thorns of no use?
Do they not make crowns for the saviors
Who sanctify and save the world?
You may not gather figs of thistles—
But I saw thistle-down volplaning
Over the orchard where the fallen figs were lying
Torpidly going to seed in their oozy sweetness.
O light-winged thoughts that scatter yourselves
Over the earth to wider harvest,
Shall I test the goodness of the tree
By the kind of fruit that I want?

## Emerson Clingman

You who are asking for friends and for a friend,
Are you sure that you are ready for a friend?
Here was myself who aspired to win for a friend
One who was notable, so long admired by me.
Then I drew near him at last and took his hand,
And he accepted me.
It turned out that he needed me,
And was waiting for me.
But I failed him,
Partly through weakness, partly through lowered devotion,
Who saw him daily now, undraped of my wonder.
And I say I had no right to seek him
Unless I could be his friend to the full!

# Wayland Reed

What way to go in the wood of this our life?
Seeking El Dorado, Beauty, I lost my path,
Wandered afar in thickets and tangled depths
Till I found a path! And what is a path but earth
Worn by the feet of other men? For the soul
Does what it dreams souls did before it, lost
In this same problem of life in the wood. What now?
Duty! loveless and sterile and hard, when Beauty
Is duty enough if Beauty be yours and courage.
Duty the path! False dream of a feeble hour,
Which leads us to mimic, walk in a way not ours.
Better to fight through briars to find the path
Made for one's soul, though lost in the darkness of fate,
Than follow steps to a mire of bitter waters—
For who can retrace?

## Rev. William Shipley

Do you know who I was, O riotous generation,
Now when thoughts and beliefs arrange themselves in no
    order of beauty,
But are pieces of broken mirror scattered upon a transient
    floor,
Reflecting no heaven, nor even the room of life?
Have you thought of me, a weary messenger of peace,
A servant in the house of God,
A heart dissolved in gospel love?
How I lived in poverty, upon the bounty of friends,
Visiting the sick, comforting the oppressed,
Counseling love, forgiveness, charity, the blameless life,
A shepherd of men to the fold of heaven?
Then brought to this humble grave and forgotten,
Lost in the weeds and sunken earth of fifty years—
Do you know what I was?

## John Bussey

Robert Fulton Tanner!
You who were bitten by a rat
While demonstrating your patent trap,
And made the rat in the trap the symbol
Of the life of you and the life of man,
Come out of your grave and view my stone,
And the metaphor that I chose:
I made it a cage and not a trap;
I made it a squirrel, and not a rat.
For a rat in a trap can only brood,
And cower awaiting the cat or tub.
But a squirrel is happy racing a cage
That keeps him racing in turn!

## Edmond Dantino

Look how the ants, the birds, the squirrels,
And the monsters of sea and land as well,
Tire, and wound themselves, and fall into traps,
And destroy each other in the endless business
Of finding food and storing up food.
But O man! O man! You give your soul
For a little food, like Lilah Prentice,
Who married an old man for his money,
Then grieved for life for the unfound mate;
And John Odell with the gift of thinking,
Who held it back while making money.
And there was myself, who almost reached
The heights of stars and blue cold air,
Compelled to descend to the valleys of food,
Or starve amid the lonely snows,
Having run out of rations!

## W. O. Morris

In the beginning God created the heavens
And the earth;
And I was born when I was born,
And died when I died—
One statement tells as much as the other!

## Reginald Payne

You are immortal, Amoeba,
Looking neither back, nor forward,
Only a dim contentment in the light of the sun!
But if every day you lived all the days of your past,
Carrying them as a wallet that galled your back:
The torture of Beauty lost, or never attained.
And if every day you lived the days to be,
Vainly trying to mold the ether of to-morrow
Into figures of victory, or delight;
And while living to-day and to-morrow
You were also living to-day,
Would you be immortal, Amoeba,
Would you not wear out?

# Warren Swinbourn

Some drift with the current,
And land amid tangled rushes, or in swamps;
Or as likely, find themselves in paradises of purple flags.
Others fight against the stream,
Yet land on the shore where the river bends.
Only a few get around to the long and final sweep.
In the next incarnation, O Fate,
Give me wisdom to swim with the stream,
Or across the stream,
In and out, in and out,
To the desired haven!

## Robert Carpenter

You were good soil, mother of me,
Mary Woolridge,
But why did you allow the poor seed of my father
To be wasted in such soil?

## Kenneth Hellhake

Passer-by. You will never know till the end
What part of you has been destined to flower,
And to become you: a red blossom, or a yellow,
A fruition of thorns and poison, or of fragrance.
Look at me: a friend of the poor at forty,
A defender of the weak, a non-resistant,
Living a life of simplicity and kindness,
But all the while loving praise more than I suspected of
    myself,
And loving money more than I suspected of myself.
Change of circumstance! And forced to abandon faiths
To win praise, being unable to live without praise;
Caught in the wreck of improvident investments,
And forced to struggle for money, I thought
So coming out at last
Not simple, faithful, clear, exalted, noble,
A pillar of fire to the people,
But a walking pawn shop sign, or barber pole;
A spiritual tramp in a tattered coat of many colors,
And patches of out-worn loves and faiths
But with bonds and stocks in a safety box,
Stored away for age, that in youth I never prized,
And scorned to reach!

## Minnie Lee

Was I different from any of you women
Of Spoon River?
Did not all of you distract attention with one hand,
While taking money from his pocket with the other hand. . . .
Not letting the right hand know what the left hand did,
Nor letting the community know it,
Nor even the victim?
Did it make any difference that you performed the trick in
    homes,
While I did it in hallways?
Did it make any difference that you did it with your
    husbands,
While I did it with gawking cattle men,
Wandering the streets after having sold their cattle,
Their pockets stuffed with twenty dollar bills?
Was my spiritual attitude any different from yours?
Did I not use benevolent animal magnetism
The same as you?

## Emma Serviss

The Canada thistle is Hate;
And Greed is a waste of weeds;
And vines that kill the oak are Envy:
And quack-grass spreading is Selfishness.
But the rose old-fashioned that climbs the trellis,
And sweetens the air of a rainy day
Is being a joy to the neighborhood,
With an open house, and an open heart,
And a hand tl.at loves to serve and lend.
And it's good in the sleep of death to dream
Of your little stone that the neighbors chiseled:
"This woman was a friend."

## Benjamin Franklin Hazard

You built the new Court House, Spoon River,
You laid one stone upon another—
But what made them stay? Was it the mortar only?
You put in arches, and groined ceilings—
What held them up? Was it the material,
Or the placing of material obedient to laws?
Who made those laws, who compelled you,
Even if you wanted neither air nor light,
Not to make vacuums of rooms, lest they collapse?
What do I mean, I who preached Americanism?
I am hitting at Americanism, laws, constitutions.
Can you make laws and constitutions the way you want to,
Against soul gravitations, arches without keys?
Rooms without air?
Or must you make them according to the laws of the soul?
What is The Law, the constitution, or the law of the soul?
What is Americanism? I tell you:
It is to be an Athenian, an Atlantian:
Free, joyous, harmonious, balanced,
Simple, just, tolerant, wise,
Peaceful, loving beauty,
Unprejudiced, seeking to learn,
Devoted to nature, and to the happiness that comes from
      these,
And a maker of new gods in the image of perfected hope,
And adoration!

## Amy Whedon

The blossoms we planted were frosted,
And black decay took them,
Until they withered into the earth.
Nothing was left but the odor of rotting stalks,
And the smell of nourished soil,
With which we strove to grow them:
Our love, and our devotion,
Our hopes and our striving labors.
All for the flower of life that we planted in vain.
Oh, my beloved, how we toiled for the life of our love!

## Henry Burman

Voices whispered to me:
Persevere, be a god!
Just among the unjust,
True among the false,
Merciful among the cruel,
Seeking the beautiful amid
Ash barrels, tin cans, hates and quarrels;
Clear visioned among the eyes that blink
In slimes and mud and sewage filth.
A little more bootless, perhaps, Spoon River
To be a god among the tree men. . . .
A little, perhaps, a little!

## Floyd Heywood

Captains and commanders,
Heroes with cannons and guns,
Have memorial statuary and gilded tombs.
Do they battle with Fear,
Disgust, Hatred, Self-Contempt,
Discouragement, and the Dishonor conferred by the world
As well as we, the obscure and unrewarded souls?
Whose bodies lie under modest head-stones like this?
Their careers are blared on a thousand pages,
While the message we leave
Is written in a language that only the wise can read.

## Stephen Spalding

Have you considered, passer-by,
That all your laws and ethics
Are founded upon the "Thou shalt nots,"
And are given for enforcement
The hateful handles of courts,
And of ostracisms, and of persecutions,
And of excommunications,
To crush into submission,
And to make into one image
The variable and fluid stuff of life?
And that if any of these "Thou shalt nots,"
With their courts and ostracisms,
Were intended to support the great "Thou shalt"
Of "Love one another,"
That the intention failed through the hatred and strife
Of enforcing the "Thou shalt nots"?
"Thou shalt not make graven images"
Has soaked the earth with blood.
"Love one another" never made a wound,
Nor dimmed an eye with sorrow!

## Robert Sincere

I built the house of my life
On the rock of invincible character,
Guarding it against the descending rains
Of regret for misspent days,
And against the floods of unrighteous living.
But an earthquake struck me:
The disaster of placing all confidence
In the integrity of man,
And in God's moral governance.
Then I saw that I should have builded
On the shifting sands of selective prudence.

## Joseph Wheelock

You didn't know, or you didn't care, you judges,
That I the car-bandit, Joseph Wheelock,
Did only what the capitalists do;
And that I acted in imitation,
And by suggestion,
And with great imagination.
Did not the banker whom I robbed and killed
Rob the township on a bond deal?
And were not the papers full of it?
You didn't indict him.
And look what you did to hang me up:
You gave my cell mate immunity
For the dirty work of winning my confidence,
And getting my story!
Your laws are only your wills
Which bend and break better laws.

## Rev. Leonard Hash

All you preachers of the Methodist, Baptist,
Presbyterian, Campbellite, and other churches—
Do you realize what you are?
You are the worm eaten seed of Isaiah and Heine,
Of Shelley and Browning;
You are dwarfed and stunted stalks of the perfect flower.
You are the runts of great breeds.
You are small souls grunting under the heavy load
Of great causes, visions and dreams,
And you make only homilies of them,
Distorting, and hiding and falsifying their reality.
You are not great souls
Uttering great causes of faith
In life and its hungers,
And making Beauty of them. . . .
How clearly I saw all this after I had committed adultery
And took to the lecture platform!

## Peter Ryan

Is it the act alone, or is it also the hate in the act
That sharpens the consequences?
Here was I prosperous, a partner of power,
Believing that I could punish my partners
For their wrong to me, by simply withdrawing,
And I withdrew.
Well, the business tangled because I left,
But what a bitter fate for me,
With lawsuits against us all,
And enemies rising up to fight me,
As helping friends to them. . . .
Poverty, isolation at last.
I went about telling I was forced out.
But I say whatever you yield to the doing,
Saying that some one caused you to do it,
Makes a common result in which you share—
Nay, of which you bear the worst!

## William Merriam

We made every sacrifice for each other;
We were wounded in every way for each other.
We enriched our love in separations,
In longings, in disappointments, in reunions,
In memories of days and nights,
And in memories of looks, smiles and tears—
We gave everything for love.
Then having made the soil of life so rich
For the blossom of love,
We were too worn to tend the flower,
To enjoy the flower.
What preparation for love! What defeat!
Save there be heaven, for which our blossom
Was ready to be transplanted!

## Myrtle Recker

What is marriage for, for children?
Well, she was barren.
What is marriage for, for nuptial delight—
But he hated her.
What is marriage for, for a home?
But she was dull and a slattern.
Yet for years he found with me
Nuptial delight, and a cosy room,
And I bore him rosy children.
Then our secret leaked, and all our pictures
Were printed in the papers.
For up rose the great Humane Society
And took my children and locked them up
By order of court in the Home of the Friendless;
And she had him arrested,
And forced him home to live with her.
So I took poison to show my hate
Of the rotten moral community.

## Mrs. Sidney Lane

It was mortifying among all the church people
And in our lovely neighborhood
To be known as a rejected wife.
Then if he went on at this rate
Out of business and living on his investments
And keeping that hussy, Mrytle Recker,
The time might come when I might want
For the very means of life,
And die for proper care of me.
Besides the man was mine, mine!
And I knew I could get him home again
By having him arrested,
And breaking the pretty love nest up.
If children are bastards it's due to sin.
And little I care that this shameless woman
Ended her life with poison.

## Priam Finish

Here I lie under the symbol of the serpent,
The intercrossed triangles, and the swastika—
A searcher of wisdom, devotee of the dogma
Of the brotherhood of man,
And one of the sons of God.
Was Jesus the only son of God?
If so, why did he not say something original?
Why did he always quote his Father's book,
Who in turn always quoted from Hammurabi,
And reiterated the words of Confucius, Mencius and Buddha?
If Jesus was the son of God why did he not write a better
       book
Than the Old Testament, or The Testament of the Twelve
       Patriarchs?
How am I to be blamed, then, for quoting,
Selecting and putting together,
Under the symbol of the serpent, the triangles and the
       swatiska?

# John Misja

So many ways and tell me what is the best:
To gain the whole world and lose your own soul;
To gain part of the world and to keep part of your soul—
Always in such case the part which moralizes and dictates,
And is paid for it.
But to lose the whole world, and to gain your own soul,
Free, pure, just loving high truths and liberties,
But enduring loneliness and poverty therefor—
That is to live by the truth,
And to die in the poorhouse as I did,
And as everyone will who gains his own soul!

## Angela Sanger

In March when the melting eaves are a prism's edge,
And icicles burn at the tips with scarlet flame,
And drip to a rataplan of chrysolites;
When the drift of a white winged cloud is over the tree tops
That lean to a flapping gale from the yellow ravine—
Then the dream of a garden returned to me, and I walked
Where the stalks of rusted sun flowers lisped the breeze.
And what were last year's failures, frosts and worms?
I would plant again for the joy of growing things;
Fight for the corn of life, for the blossoms of beauty.
And with every spring with a heart that never tired,
The dream of winning a love that should thrive, be free
Of cares that choke, betrayals that break, or doubts
That chill the leaves put forth to a sanguine sun!
O, garden by which I lived! O, earth of my heart!
How was it enriched by the fallen stalks of hope?
What did I gather but strength to struggle in Springs
Of the blue sky thrill of the dream?

# *Jacob Mordant*

Looking forward with rapt delight
To the day of riches and a great house,
I labored and saved until I was fifty.
Then with my money boxes full,
And my great house built,
I said: "Soul, take thy ease,
Thou hast food for many days."
In that very moment my soul was required of me:
I neither knew the house, nor could I enjoy the riches
With that soul of me which remained,
After winning them
With the soul which was gone!

## The Poncey Children

Here we are, five of us,
Children of William and Janis Poncey.
All of us are nameless, for none of us lived a day:
Three of us died in an hour,
One in two hours, one in five.
And all of our little stones are alike,
And contain nothing but dates and the parentage;
And in a circle carved at the top
A passion flower bent upon its broken stalk.
Why does the old maid Zetta Tucker
Come here so often, and kneel before our stones,
And look and look?

## Laura Santini

He was at least thirty-five,
And I was fifteen—
And he kept looking at me,
Looking at me whenever we met.
One day while he was looking at me
I saw the vision of celestial beauty in his eyes.
Beholding him thus so bewitched
By mortality as plain as mine,
And remembering the hole in my stocking
I smiled at him.
In that moment I comprehended
Why Beatrice smiled on Dante!

## Robert Chain

There are two ways in life,
And I tried them both:
First a life of no change,
Life like a gull, which has no dream
But to be a gull, fly over the waters,
Seeking its food, and to nest and sleep!
And then I became a creature that nurses
Growth and mutation in the brain,
Swims to land and turns its fins to legs.
Sensing a shriveled life ahead,
And loathing the weary hour,
I changed myself to renew myself,
And lost myself!

## Hagard Pihlblad

Listen, you infidels and pantheists,
And maudlin sentimentalists,
Talking a God of love;
And saying that man, as bad as he is,
Would never create eternal hell,
So how could a God of love do so,
And doom to eternal punishment
The wretched children of men?
Poor simpletons! Didn't your God of love
Create Life and the World?

## Dulany Levering

Whatever you say of me, Spoon River,
None of you can truly declare
That I did not live my life
With uncomplaining endurance.
Did you help each other?
Did you carry the cross of Jesus,
And whine about your own?
Yet it was he who said:
"Whosoever doth not bear his own cross
Cannot be my disciple."

## Fremont Flack

Carve for me a spindle
Upon which my intestines are being wound,
As they did in the days of the Inquisition.
Who is winding the spindle?
Don't you know? Let it go!


## Ignatius Marlowe

Imprison the eagle with the crows,
Who know not what the eagle knows,
He will croak a little when crowded,
Or whistle when his soul is clouded.
But free him back to be with the eagles,
How he flaps his wings and shrieks,
When the lightning the heaven streaks,
And all the peaks call to the peaks!

## Victor Chambers

After your scheme of the people's salvation is defeated,
And your life is defeated in that defeat,
There are two courses to pursue:
One is to drink and drown away,
Harming no one but yourself, if yourself.
The other is to let the bitterness of defeat
Arm your life with malice,
And spur you to fresh endeavors
For laws, measures, retaliations,
In punishment of the world which rejected you.
That was I, Spoon River,
Masking my energized hatred
With activity for the public weal!

## Chandler Nicholas

Every morning bathing myself and shaving myself,
And dressing myself.
But no one in my life to take delight
In my fastidious appearance.
Every day walking, and deep breathing
For the sake of my health.
But to what use vitality?
Every day improving my mind
With meditation and reading,
But no one with whom to exchange wisdoms.
No agora, no clearing house
For ideas, Spoon River.
Seeking, but never sought;
Ripe, companionable, useful, but useless
Chained here in Spoon River,
My liver scorned by the vultures,
And self-devoured!

## Nast Nicholas

And the truths I meant to speak truly
Proved untrue.
All the prophecies of ill and disaster
Spoken by me were never fulfilled.
All the characters I denounced,
And tried to write down,
Remained upright, and stand to-day
Fairer and brighter of fame.
Is it not good to be forgotten?
Remembrance of me would be remembrance
Of my vision untrue, my tongue that strayed.
All is well as it is . . . all is well.
Oblivion, just friend, kind friend!

## Albert Thurston

Who lives where the eagle lives?
The lizard!
The lizard crawls at the feet of the eagle.
Who lives where the eagle lives?
The snake!
The snake is coiled by the eagle's nest!
Who soars where the eagle soars?
The vulture!
The condor!
But who clasps the crags in the lonely heights,
With the sunlight on his golden wings,
Crowned with the planet of morning?—
The eagle!

# *Lottie Chipp*

Am I the only slave whose clothes were taken
In a house of shame?
How about the wife who sticks for bread?
How about the poor minister who has changed his creed,
But has a family?
How about the editorial writer
Compelled to lie, too old to get out?
How about some of your great authors
Unable to forsake an habitual comfort?
How about the publishers, splendid madams of exploitation,
Owning the copyrights, the clothes of poor writers?
All are inmates, or keepers of houses—
Everyone loses her clothes!

# Covington Chance

Assassin! Relentless Fiend!
He will find you, kill you at last,
Wherever you are, whatever you do!
I hoped to dodge him, if not escape him,
But I had to sleep, and he caught me asleep,
He came like a thief in the night.
And I suddenly opened my eyes to see
A figure had entered,
Stood back to me,
Was softly locking the door again,
And hiding the key somewhere in his cloak.
He was dressed in tights all woven in rhombes,
Some black as coal, some red as blood.
And the cloak that hung from one of his shoulders
Was figured with signs of the zodiac,
Sprinkled with beetles, lambs and crosses,
Torches, ibises, amaranth.
And over his eyes was a demi-mask,
Such as the headsman wears.
I sat up in the strength of sudden terror,
Preparing to fight him.
But he fell on me like a drift of cloud or smoke.
Darkness! starred by the point of a silver dagger—
A little pain—that's all!

## *Wilbur Noble*

If friends or wedded ones may quarrel,
And become friends again,
Finding something sweeter than they had before,
Do you not understand how I,
Pierced with many bullets at the battle of Shiloh,
And dying a prisoner of war,
Felt the highest love
When nursed and embraced at last
By a soldier of the enemy?

## Virgil Chubb

Was it not hard enough to write my poems,
According to my vision,
And against the constant opposition of my wife,
Who was forcing her beliefs and her pieties upon me,
Without having her at last influence my expression
In spite of all my will?
Is it not hard enough to have an enemy,
Without having to feed and live with that enemy?
If these things are merely tests of character
And to be borne with a brave smile,
How would you like to be sued for alimony,
And have your copyrights taken from you in payment?
Is this enough? Can you stand some more?
Very well!
How would you like to have your wife survive you,
And publish a collected edition of your poems
From which everything you ever wrote
According to your vision was excluded;
And everything which she influenced you to write
Was included?
Would you turn in your grave?
Or would you still smile the brave smile?

## *Milo Fornshell*

I stood for the creed that would have saved
The liberty and the forward step
Of the city, state and the nation:
The rule of affairs by the greatest numbers,
With the greatest knowledge and interest.
But the rattle of pie pans wearied you;
And you followed the lure of the far away,
Till now you have the smallest numbers,
With the smallest knowledge, and smallest interest
Headed by clerks and notary publics
Who pull the strings of your jumping jacks
In a bureau in Washington, and quick
Mayors dance in the Philippines,
And governors in Texas.

## Joseph Nightingale

I busied my youth with study:
Statistics, economics, theories of government,
How to control the railroads, and public utilities;
I worshipped before the shrine of Marx,
Engels, La Salle, Altgeld,
And noisy writers of pamphlets
On taxation, prohibition and social reform.
I burned candles to Shelley as reformer,
And to John Brown as martyr;
And I made saints of the fanatics of millenniums,
Not dreaming that none of them was for liberty,
But only for the idea that possessed them.
Then after twenty years everything changed:
The statistics were no longer true;
The economics had withered with the passing years,
Even as the evils they denounced had vanished with time—
All of this, just as I saw that truth is Art,
Not fact, statistics, argument,
Or pounding the rich, or making laws.
Then Art alone could solace me,
If I had known it enough to be solaced!

## Merritt Larkin

That picture of me hung in the Public Library
Shows me wise and strong,
Fortunate and happy,
As if living a rounded and harmonious life.
But if you can see behind the face of great Beethoven
To the little tangles, the miserable cares,
The daily tortures that are belied by that godlike brow,
And those masterful eyes,
You can well believe that that picture of me
Hides the much that fell short,
And the increasing littleness of my life!

## Leo Gallian

I never had a mother, so I fell—
So said Alta Dance.
I never had a mother, so I rose,
Said I at the end of life.
For what are relatives but clinging roots
Of a growth entwined, but of hostile life?
And what is a mother but life that sends
Blood in your veins that has lived its day?
I cut the maternal cord and fled;
I fell as much as Alta Dance;
But I rose from the fall, and rising became
Triumphant and myself!

## Mary Nolen

Children commence on the schoolyard
To talk and torment each other about that.
Some little girl or little boy is driven to daily torture
For fingers pointed and accusing giggles about that.
It is always that to the day of one's death.
It is known that nothing can be told about another
That will hurt and tangle like telling about that.
Women give that and then are mocked by the one to whom
    they give it,
And the whole town takes up the hue and cry.
Money is given to hush the talk about that;
Fights and murders are about that;
Wills are made and revoked because of that;
Shrugs, laughs, accusations are about that.
Reputations, fortunes, go to pieces because of that,
And one half of the woe of the world is about that.
What is that, that it should produce
Shame, terror, crime, ruin and crucifixion
All over America?

## Rafael Chernetti

I scrubbed the floor of Doctor Peffer,
But as he wouldn't pay me,
I sent him a dun on a postal card,
A prison offense as it seems,
Although I didn't know it.
Well, they convicted me and jailed me,
Although I appealed and won at last,
Because the judge was wrong in his charge
To the jury on the law.
Nevertheless I was broken and died.
Ignorance of the law excuses no man—
Unless he is a judge.

## Oscar Fellonneau

Perfect Creation! The eye not fitted to its end.
The veriform appendix useless, dangerous!
Sex! Woman a flame
Out of the volcanic furnaces of nature;
Man but kindling, quickly consumed—
A million, million tragedies here.
And myself! grown flaccid of flesh,
Still shaken by violent desire,
Until I was mad; and in revenge
Of nature, and my own impotence
Was caught in that nameless act.
You are perfect, O Nature—
But only by saying man's tragedy
Mars not your great perfection!

## Jacob Farmer

Barry Holden! First apple to fall from the gallows tree
In Spoon River!
Little did I think as a boy, listening in horror
To the tale of your crime from my father's lips
That I, too, should dangle from that tree,
Understanding you, as the noose was looped for me.
Why is the slow killing of a man ignored,
And the quick killing of a man punished?
And the slow killing of a man shut from view
Of the courts that look through a tube called the law,
Pointed straight at the murderer's face?
Through years and years the wretch I killed
Waited and watched, plotted and followed,
Until at last he grabbed my farm
By the law of the land, by the broken law of right,
He was killing me by inches.
And what I did was to turn as a cornered wolf
That tears the hunter!

## August Matson

I was the sheriff of Spoon River
Who noosed the neck of Jacob Farmer.
And I watched the people for days before
Greedily awaiting the horrible hour;
While the newspapers howled like tigers for blood.
Then on the day there were the crowds around the jail,
Hungry for the dead body to be brought from the gallows.
O you people of Spoon River,
Jacob Farmer is in his grave,
The murder in his heart is quenched,
But you go on brutalizing yourselves,
Asking for the strangled bodies with cold and deliberate
        malice
From behind the painted masks of Justice and Law.
You brutalized yourselves through Jacob Farmer
To deal as a murderer
With murderers to come!

## Leigh Dickinson

Come! Children of dreams and crusts,
Come! and learn the joy of keeping,
The peril of losing your dreams and crusts.
For I blasphemed the faith of the artist:
I left my jeans for a cut-a-way;
Left my people, and left my stories;
Left my poverty, strove for money;
Courted the tables of prominent bankers,
And drank their wine for the wine of life.
O ears of Midas hairy and long,
Too late I found them grown to my head,
Perched in middle class splendor at last;
Or blinking under the lights of the city,
My star all lost, and nearly forgotten,
That rested over my manger!

## Isabel, William and Albert

Soul of the Universe! Eternal Love!
Making for change and death—but for life!
Multiform, mysterious, exhaustless,
Is it not through you that our spirits became one—
A bond in the flesh on earth,
And mingled flames in this realm?
We three, lovers, husbands of the same woman!
First I, this woman that was,
Who loved William and was his wife,
And loved him none the less in death,
Nor less when I became the wife
Of you, my adored Albert;
Next I, this man William,
Who loved you, Albert, in life,
And next in death
Because you loved the Isabel I loved.
And lastly, I who was Albert,
Who loved you, William, because you loved her,
Because she loved you,
I, who was her husband to the last,
Treasuring your memory with her—
Being, O blissful fate, what you were to her,
With something else which spoke for progress in love.
This is the mystery, the final consummation,
The illumination of passion,
The realization of eternal light
From the love of man and woman on earth!

# Jack Kelso

To rear, to watch, to lose;
To be the soul of a sailor's wife: to wait.
To be a workman with adze and plane,
And to see your finished ship sail off,
And to know it no more;
To hear of the storms it weathered, the ports it reached.
To live here to the day of my death,
With the old things we had together, he and I:
The fiddle, the tramps by the river,
The rod and the gun,
And Shakespeare under a tree.
While he was commanding armies,
And wresting laws from mountains cloven asunder
By lightning and earthquakes,
To remain a fisherman and a fiddler;
But living days of wonder
About my storm embattled chum;
And wondering if I ever knew him,
And if I were I!

## Stephen A. Douglas

What were we doing in those days of my life,
Building a temple, or steering a ship?
And, therefore, what was our law,
The north star, or a light house?
Were we lifting colossal stones into place
Or driving pegs for the ropes of a sheltering tent?
As for me, I know:
I thought of Liberty for a great race,
Even though it trampled justice to a small race.
I pushed ahead for an ocean bound republic,
While radicals paused to straighten paths
For the weary feet of the weak.
Then the ocean for me, and waves unknown,
I who had outlived the laws of the land;
And a heaven that veiled its guiding lights,
To me the Titan, sensing deeper laws
Than those of the rill that turns a little wheel.
There will be an era of clear skies
When the north star shows again.
Will it shine over a temple builded
To the phase of a passing noon,
In the days when I shall be constellated with Caesar?

## D'Arcy Singer

What is the life of a man,
What is the life of the race,
O friends of Spoon River?
It is that creation out of the spirit of man
Of statuary, pictures, temples, the written page,
Laws and states,
Ideals of Joy and Fellowship.
Humanism, Balance, Beauty.
These are man's creations and creators.
These are the webs of the spider
Woven out of his own body;
These are the combs of the bees
Gathered from life's flowers and architected.
These are the nests of the eagles enduring a century!

# Celestine Conant

Daughter of Edith Conant
Who sang with thrilling sorrow the morn of my birth.
All my life long holding up the torch of Beauty
In Spoon River,
And most of Spoon River passing by;
Some blind, some with eyes, but jeering.
Some opposing. And even the friends of my torch
Busy with their lamps and candles.
And then the party they gave me;
The final recognition, the acclaim:
The blind pretending that they saw,
And the jeerers praising!
Just one hour of triumph,
And the ecstasy too much,
Never found till then, not to last,
My years being spent.
Next day death.
Who will take up my torch ere the dust quench it?

## Emilius Poole

Did you ever see a growth,
Whether of flower or weed,
Break down and waste because of excess of life?
That was I, fellow citizens,
With no work to employ my restless energies,
And fulfill my vision of life.
Say you that the right man finds his work?
What would have become of General Grant
If the war had not come on?
He was sinking into decay,
And was rescued miraculously for himself and the country
By the opportunity of the war.
But no war came for me!

## Rivers McNaughton

If water cannot rise higher than its source,
Can it be clearer than its banks?
Did you ever notice the difference
Between Big Creek and Spudaway?
One runs clear water over pebbly bottoms,
The other slush between the corn belt's
Dark and friable soil;
Yet both are fed by springs from the hills.
The source of my soul was pure,
And the urge of my soul was pure.
But the caving banks of desperate days
Muddled my waters, that swirled and hastened
In dreams of the crystal depths of the sea,
Under an earthless sky!

## Lucius Clute

Lillian, with her whims,
Her tangled complexes,
And changeable ways;
And little disharmonies with herself,
And with me;
And her teasing charms, and ruddy hair,
And adorable breasts,
Was the woman for me in the days of my strength,
When any lesser woman mystery
Could not have held me—
Me the betrayer, and flyer, and deserter!
But oh! in the days of my decline
How her whims and complexes
Wore me down;
And how her teasing charms exhausted me,
And tortured me, bestowed on another
In the days of my decline!

# Imanuel Reedy

Not you, son of Joseph and Mary,
The carpenter's son, the ax at the root of the tree;
Not you, Jesus of Nazareth,
The wonder worker, and healer of the blind;
Not you, the offspring of David,
Preaching sedition against Caesar;
Not you the King of the Jews,
Restorer of the throne, the power of Israel;
Not you, the consolation of Judah,
The mediator, the propitiation, the judge, the rabbi;
Not you, the stone of stumbling, the head of the church;
Not you, whose words and works
Are the substance of customs and creeds,
And that law which you uprooted, but which grew again;
Nor even you the friend of publicans and harlots,
The feaster, the liver, the sweet companion;
Nor even you the firstfruits of them that are asleep—
But you, the son of God, the man of sorrows,
The vine and the witness
Of youth's swift dream, and manhood's lingering pain,
And faith whose root is dead but lives again;
You the symbol of immemorial betrayal,
The agony fulfilled, the occult sacrifice;
You, the High Priest of the Greater Mysteries,
Of birth and death and life renewed,
Ritualist of the rose of Sharon, the song of the morning star,
Fulfiller of the law of the soul;
You, the Word that was with God, and is made flesh;
Great Seal of the martyrdom of man, you the cross,
The hieroscript of Life. . . .
O ineffable Christ!

## *Lionel Grierson*

How often in our chamber, O adored one,
I woke to see the midnight star, and find you
Warm and sweet as incense, hear your breathing;
Feel the dreaming love of your constant breast.
Then in the throes of death to suffer absence,
And wait for you, and wait for you in vain,
And from our bed—how cold with death and sorrow
To see the star of midnight—what remembrance!
Arielle! Lay your head on this earthen pillow,
Touch my hand of dust with the dust of your hand;
Warm this couch with the passion of your presence;
Sleep by my side forever and give me rest!

## Arielle Grierson

Heartbroken that I could not reach your bed side
In those last hours; heartbroken that death took you,
Soon I came to you, soon to your earthen couch.
Sleep now and rest, I am here. The star of midnight
Over us watches, as once in our chamber of life.
My dust has the April longing to turn and mingle
With yours, which longs for mine. What flowers shall blossom
With the color of primal passion from such a union!

## Judge Singleton

You never knew, Spoon River,
Why it was that I exonerated Amos Winkler
From the charge of perjury,
Swearing for the sake of more pension money
That Charles Winkler was his son,
When in truth he was the illegitimate son
Of another man, before Amos married the mother.
Amos was kind to the boy, and was raising him,
Even as I loved the daughter of my wife,
The natural child of another man—
(A fact not known to you, Spoon River),
Before I married the mother!

## Samuel Delafield

She adored me at first;
She blushed and stammered in my presence at first;
She praised my strength and knelt to my power at first.
And then gradually she was more at ease,
Less worshipful, and a little critical,
Until she treated me as an equal,
And then as her possession, her servant.
And do you know what it means?
Every woman is a Delilah, who cannot rest,
And never stops until she knows the secret
Of the strong man's strength.
And she will tell his secret to all the world
And belittle him to the populace,
If he tries to escape her.

## *Eva Hopewell*

You! The sophisticated of Spoon River
Mocked my stories of the happy ending,
And would have none of me.
And all the while you were wondering and moaning
Because your own lives did not have the happy ending—
And expecting it, too!
You were little cynics after all,
Doubting the happiness never yours.
And not only hunting those who were happy,
But howling against the story of any
Happiness never yours!

## James Istel

After you have lived and read many books;
And fathomed Patience, Courage, Friendship, Love,
Through suffering and experience.
And seen how much of hate there is in the world, and why;
And how much of robbery there is in the world and why;
And how much of slander there is in the world and why;
And how much of malice, selfishness and cruelty there is
    in the world and why;
And after so living you have also learned your age,
Then if you cannot make understandable what you know;
And if the new generation is not interested in what you know,
Are you not buried alive and epitaphed with hieroglyphics?
And are you not the voice of wisdom
Which never yet has bequeathed much of its lore
To the next era?

## Gerald Loveman

My daughter disobeyed me,
And eloped with the man I hated.
And that began the fateful sequence
That brought me here.
But when the mists cleared up from my mind,
As the heat of earth and life grew cool,
I saw that it wasn't merely this man,
But that I should have hated any man
Whom she desired in the marriage embrace,
And who desired her!

# Prof. Mackemeyer

My poverty and suffering and illness at last
Were not due to the sin of running away
With Professor Gardner's wife.
But they followed link by link upon
The act of my wife in bringing to court
My so-called crime of running away;
And link by link upon
The ostracism of the good,
And the active malice of enemies,
Who took occasion to wreak their hatred,
That never had had a handle before.
And seeing all this I stripped away
The parrot clatter of moralists:
The Greek tragedies are not studies in Fate,
Nor in the wrath of God—
They are studies in human revenge!

## Julian Starring

By the sentence of the angels they cursed me—
It didn't hurt.
They execrated me in the presence of the sacred books—
I didn't mind.
They anathematized me with the anathema
With which Joshua anathematized Jericho—
Very well.
They heaped upon me the maledictions
That Elisha poured upon the children—
No bears, that I could see.
They invoked the wrath of the Lord to burn me—
But I kept cool.
They petitioned the Lord to blot my name from heaven—
That was too far ahead and away to worry about.
But when they cursed me when lying down,
And cursed me when rising up
And cursed me when going out or coming in;
And demanded that no man speak to me,
Or stay under the same roof with me,
Or come near me,
Or give me work—
Then I starved, then I died!

## Heraclitus Procrustes

Franklin sent a kite into the heavens,
And brought down electricity to men.
Follow me, friends of Spoon River,
Send the X-ray and your thought
Into the electron and bring thence God.
As my namesake of old believed,
So I believe:
Fire is the soul of the universe,
The primal and only substance—
Πάντα ῾ρεῖ.

## Tennyson Repplier

Adored one!
In what far place are you sleeping?
While my dust wastes here,
And wasting cries for yours.
How we strove in life
To eternalize our hours of ecstasy,
Even as Peter would build tabernacles
On the mountain of transfiguration!
And shall we neither tell of our hours together,
Nor understand them till the resurrection?

## Bessy Works

Do not some of you earn your bread as merchants,
And live your real life with the violin or the pen?
Even so, I married John for a living,
And kept Charles for love.
Can you prove any real evil against me
Without also proving
That a pen is evil, or love is evil.

# William Low

Here lies the body of William Low.
After his death it was known
That in order to save his friend,
Who was guilty,
He endured imprisonment,
Being himself innocent,
But in his strength believing
That he could endure walls and bars
Better than his friend.
This stone is erected by Father Ambrose Murphy,
The priest of Spoon River;
And by John Burchard
The grog-keeper.

## *Norris Littell*

I moved from a better house to a better house,
I built the house of my desire,
And lived in the house for years and years
While Stuart Herring was building his house,
And all the while was adding to it;
First a porch and then a window,
According to fancy from time to time,
And having his wish in a kind of growth,
And never achieving it, always expectant
Of wonders yet to be.

## Stuart Herring

At forty-five I married and had a son—
He would be of age when I was near seventy.
At forty-five I grew prosperous and built a house.
At fifty I was more prosperous still,
And wrecked my house and rebuilt my house—
Always at least ten years late.
Then money losses and vexations:
The bay window one year, a little plastering the next,
And a part of the porch the next,
Determined to finish the house.
Sixty years of age and the house not done,
Habituated now to living in an unfinished house,
And even the design forgotten by which I would rebuild it!

## Prue and Luella

Here lies between us two
Our beloved husband, Nicholas.
He is indifferent, we are not jealous;
The town is not scandalized,
For we take no delight together.
O Death! of all the grave smiles
You have carved in this place
None is more smiling than ours!

# Father Alan Drinkwater

If man shall not live by bread alone,
Shall he live by the faith that brings him bread?
If man shall live by every word that proceedeth out of the
    mouth of God,
Shall he not live by love, God's favorite word?
Did I sin by resigning the ministry
And marrying the woman I loved?
Did I cause her to commit adultery?
I couldn't believe it,
And I believed it less,
As I loved her more,
Amid the hate and the persecution
Of Bible ruled Spoon River!

## Abram Stein

David, sweet singer of Israel,
Did you not also smite Goliath to death
With a rock from your terrible sling?
And if I sang no songs, Spoon River,
Worthy your remembrance,
I was your satirist,
Your voice of outraged beauty,
Smiting Ignorance and Greed,
And Hatred and Hypocrisy,
To the day of my death!

## Mason Moist

Passer-by! If you walk wisely in life
You will come to belief in every word of the Bible,
And turn from foolish tenderness and faith in man
To contempt and doubt of the race.
Did not God once destroy the world with flood?
And why not with fire on the judgment day?
The universe needs cleansing with fire
Of the worthless litter and stench of man—
And God will see to that!

## Philip Dever

I made my way from the time I was fourteen,
I educated myself.
I married, earned a house, built up a fortune.
I sent the children away to school,
I safeguarded them against my hardships.
I spread too rich a feast before them:
They rushed from dish to dish,
In a disconcerted hurry to taste of everything.
Now this obelisk which they put up in gratitude.
Carve this for me:
"Raised to Philip Dever
By the generation which he didn't foresee."

## U. S. Stopp

Walking in town, a little drunk,
I saw from the road the humble stone
Of Isaac Waite, which said "I. Waite"
And I read the words, "Thy will be done,"
As "You will be done."
And then and there I laughed and chose
That epitaph, "You will be done,"
Which, passer-by, you see!

## Stella Sturgis

Is it not written: "Fear not them which kill the body,
But are not able to kill the soul.
But rather fear him which is able
To destroy both soul and body."
Was it not you, O Anson Inglish,
Who killed that soul of me that rejoiced and smiled,
And trusted and believed in both you and the world?
And gave me sorrowing and tears,
And doubt in their stead?
And sunk my body and soul in the paths of a hell
Of useless days and broken health?

# Frances Cordell

What a moment of strange dying! Quickly
All my vision girdled earth and showed me
Temples in far India, tombs in Persia,
Down the Appian way, and over Florence,
Home of Dante, wandering place of Browning.
And how strange, how prying was the vision:
For the coffin of old Landor opened;
Showed me what was left of that imperious,
Proud and lonely singer of strange beauty.
There he lay, gone down to bits of nothing—
Just a few stray hairs, a piece of shoulder,
Nothing else of him who wrote these verses:
"Proud word you never spoke, but in some future
Day you will keep not speaking of me these words,
Over my open volume you will linger,
You will say in reading: 'This man loved me.' "
Who was she and where is gone her beauty?
In what place of cypress or of willows,
In what separation from her poet,
Lies the woman, never speaking proud words?
Only these, as I have said while reading:
"This man loved me," tears upon the pages!

## Douglas Strong

I used to orate in Proctor's Grove:
I care more for the sacred principles
Of local self-government
Than all the niggers in Christendom.
Now a negro owns and lives
In my mansion house by the river.
And the scrawny son of A. D. Blood,
Who married my daughter, has named his son
Eighteenth Amendment Blood!

## Henry Ditch

As a boy old bachelors and old maids
Were pointed out to me as hearts of ideal devotion
Consecrated to the memory of a lost love,
Or a departed love.
It was not that, as I learned for myself,
That kept their souls from marriage:
If the sun of March brings April breezes,
And tempts the blossoms forth
To the numbing fingers of sudden frost,
And the flail of bitter snow,
The soul of the tree sinks down exhausted,
And cannot bud again.
And that is love forced back by fear,
And robbed of its power to try again
In life's precarious garden!

# Piper Divilbliss

As I had studied dietetics
I knew the effect of carbohydrates;
And what the proteids did and caffein,
And the ruin gluttony plays with the kidneys,
And whether a man should feed or starve.
Yet I served them eggs and served them meat,
As much as they wanted and could pay for,
As once old Burchard sold them beer,
Until they hadn't a nickel.
And what was the difference in morals, tell me,
Between the seller of booze and myself,
Except that caffein isn't whiskey.
And roast beef isn't beer?

## Eleanor Powell

First the loss of my little son—
Inconsolable grief, it seemed.
Then as one passes on the train from the familiar town
To a strange country,
Change, forgetfulness of the old scenes,
So his death became one of the memories,
Even a peace.
Loss of fortune, the vanishment of friends,
Health gone, and suffering,
Followed by quietism—
Life at last wipes all our tears away!

## Aristotle Dolegg

Carve for me the word Ephphatha,
Which is to say: Be opened.
What miracle did Christ most often perform?
The casting out of the devil of dumbness.
What causes the most suffering in the world?
Our dumb hearts that cannot make themselves
Understood of each other.

## Butler Tracy

If self-expression be an end,
And song be an end,
Then suffering, since it gives the subjects for song
Is to a good end.
But who was ever able to express
All the wisdom
Gained from suffering?
And to what end was the wisdom
For which I found no words?

# Lusk Illington

One life at a time, one world at a time,
One dream for working out in life—
But, oh, the price we pay, my friends,
For the coveted achievement!
For as to the mating of bodies and souls,
The planting of your garden,
For food and delight in life,
It comes to an idiosyncrasy
If you stop to think it over:
It's eyes of gray, or eyes of blue,
It's a certain mouth, or color of hair,
It's a nose that calls to something in you;
That is the woman for me.
And then you get the eyes, or nose,
And that is all you get.
And I who wanted a woman for wife—
Star-like, clear and pure,
Followed the instinct till I got her.
And what was she? She was pure, no doubt—
But so is filtered water!

## Benjamin Lander

Flame! the color of it, shape and power
Who knows while it flickers to the wind?
Flames on the hearth mount high
Because of pitch and resin.
They soar, entwine, flame wrestles with flame.
But the bed of coals is a steady glow:
And thus I never knew myself till desire,
Ambition, lust of the world were burned away,
And the will of me urging itself to mount,
Leaving my essential self
Like carbon, the basis of life,
Seeing calmly, all coals at last!

# Belle Dollinger

Sisters! Fellow citoyens!
You of the homes, society, the little and great life!
Married ladies! Precious rubies of the faith of virtue!
Is there only one sin, and that one fornication?
Is not lying a sin, and even lying about fornication a sin?
Do you ever burden your husbands with bills?
Do you ever deceive your husbands about the bills?
Do you ever loaf on your jobs as home keepers and mothers?
Do you know much? Do you teach the children much?
Do you love the beautiful? Are you even clean of body,
To say nothing of mind?
And don't you have little affairs sometimes?
Didn't some of you have them before you were married,
And fool your bridegrooms with the pretense of virginity?
And you, the unmarried, leading impeccable lives
To the outward world,
Do not some of you have affairs, all so secret,
And yet cheat the man who thinks himself solely favored?
Scared to death of exposure as to the man who loves you,
Yet willing to have a secret fault as to the man who loves you.
Pure to the outer world,
Rotten in the inner world of your soul.
And I! Who did not know about me?—
All of you held your skirts when passing me.
Yet sisters! Fellow citoyens!
An honest whore's the noblest work of God!

## Job Howes

Barley straws to an eastern wind,
So are the minutes to the minutes.
This restless hour hunts the hour that hides,
To-morrow draws to-day.
And as for me not pain alone
For the toppling minutes that toppled the minutes,
But that which whispered: Doing this?
What is it that you are neglecting?
What chance are you missing, and what's forgotten.
You search this way, should it be that?
And always in the middle forehead
Disquiet for the voice which said:
Move on faster, hurry! hurry!
And never a right to make reply:
"Tarry till I come."

## Peter Van Loon

Jesus and the mystical faith ruined me,
Spoon River!
For caught in an unendurable place in life
I endured for the sake of my soul's triumph:—
Forgiving daily those who forged and guarded
The cell of my fate day after day.
They profited by my sufferings and struggles.
Whilst I exhausted by the battle for soul triumph
Had no strength left for life
After I had triumphed.

## Frederick Falls

Autumnal bonfire of fallen and failing days!
But they put out the fire, my wife and son,
And little Clare, my stenographer,
Who lighted the fire, then walked away
With the torch and would not light it again,
All so chaste, but hinting the while
Of marriage, could I be free.
They stamped on my fire till all was ashes,
Ashes and dust: a stroke and a chair,
In which I was wheeled by little Clare,
Who read me the Bible, and asked me to trade
The love of God for love of her,
And saying I'd walk again if I'd take
The gift of God and give her up
I saw what it was: she loved my son,
Young and soon to inherit my wealth.
Well, I didn't give up, nor believe, nor walk.
I sat to the end where they had gummed me
In a sick aesthetic and sicker ethic,
Beaten by Nature's God!

# Henry Ivins

All my life long I could see
That the struggle for bread produced envy,
Hatred, strife, wars, disease.
And that the failures, corroded with envy,
Turned to atheism, and accepted life
As chaos and chance.
But when I came to die I saw this truth:
Settle the matter of bread,
Remove that envy from life,
And you have left the envy of the soul,
That some souls are more acceptable to God
Than your soul is.
And I say to you that in ages to be
When the matter of bread is solved for all,
And this earth becomes a battleground of souls
For favor with God—
What murders, what suffering, what tragedy for this!

## Algot Lancor

Stranger! They will come to you
And counsel you against bitterness.
But if the wine be wholly gone,
And the dregs remain in the cup,
Wherewith shall the cup be sweetened?

## *Joseph Donnelly*

If self-sacrifice were only the rescuing of people
From plights in which you have had no part—
Alas! it is also the rescuing
Of people from plights against which you have warned
    them.
Here was I, who fought to keep my daughter away
From the man she married;
Then sharing with her the misfortune that came
From marrying the man,
And losing my fortune and health through him
To the end of voiceless dust,
And my incommunicable secret!

## David Duty

Cut and thrashed and left in the field,
And therefore brooding upon the summer, and growing days.
Taking the rains of loneliness,
Enduring the August skies of blinding revelations;
Solitary in the field of life, and sinking down;
Getting the mildews;
Fermenting between moisture and heat;
Bursting in flames at last in a great rebellion
Against the decay of life . . .
Seek and end it, friends,
In the leaping passion of flowers.
Fly the fire of the rotting straw stack,
Consumed by its own disgust!

# Conrad Herron

I wrote no book, Spoon River;
I left no library to you;
I endowed no school for you;
My face is not embossed in bronze
In the court-house corridor,
As the faces are of Editor Whedon,
And Thomas Rhodes, the banker.
But did I do nothing for you,
Did I leave you no legacy?
Is it worth nothing to you
That dying with cancer
I endured with fortitude and patience?

## Marcus Jarissen

Why did I become a wanderer?
It was to get different views of the same thing,
Even of you, Spoon River!
Why did I become a wanderer?
To get new views of things never before known!
And even to sing old songs in my wanderings
Was to give them new tones and meanings,
According to the sky that was over me,
And the land that was about me!

## Stanley Lockhardt

I was one whose presence in the world
Awoke the psychotropic power of an enemy,
Subtle and tireless.
He came first with gifts, but with sinister smiles.
He was unobtrusive, but always to be sensed,
And always appeared at some critical hour.
He emerged to look me through, to make notes.
Absent he kept track of me, knew my movements,
Successes, reverses.
In the hour of my greatest triumph
He sat in the audience, his eyes bright with envy,
His lips horned with dispraise.
In the silences of life he would appear,
As one might awake from sleep to find a python's head
Reared to one's face, and staring.
I lost him at last, he seemed to be gone for good.
But my fabric crumbled. Disaster came—
Then he arrived to complete my ruin—
Why was it?

## C. Lytton

Is the ground cursed for the sake of man?
Are thorns and thistles a curse?
And is it a curse to eat your bread
In the sweat of your face?
Well, anyway what a race believes
They put as a curse in the mouth of God.
And you couldn't expect us to be farmers
With the Bible that curses the land and work,
And a stock behind us that loved the bank,
Prospering in the city.

## Philip Earling

All of my beauty of person withered at last,
All of my gifts come down to the little gift
Of telling of days of my life and their vanished dreams,
Sweet as wild honey, they said, with the wisdom of age.
To what end, gods of the far-flung mysteries,
Did I hear great music before this birth in Spoon River,
And never on earth could abide the music of earth?
And why remembered visions of crystal ranges,
And meadows of light,
Coming to me in my little life of duty—
Me the dreamer of domes to be, the mighty,
Caught in a karma of sacrifice and labor
For bread for a brood, in a fight with Greed and Envy?
Was I a serpent banished from paradise?
Or a man predestined to be the brother of Michael,
Drawn up from the mire to stars by music and dreams?
Calling me ever and never giving me rest?
I was blind at last, but the inner eye pierced through
The fogs of earth to heaven! And now what music!
Above all music that ever was heard on earth,
In tune with the tides of the sea, and the bell of the buoy
That rose and fell with the mile long waves and gathered
With sound and swell the light of the sinking sun!

## Thomas Nelson

There were two supreme moments in my life:
First when amid applause
I ascended the platform of power
As president of the county board.
Second, when I sat alone, ill, half speechless,
In an ante-room, before the beginning
Of my successor's inaugural.
And there in that moment of passing out
To have Henry Cabanis,
Who had fought me all my term,
And defeated my plan for good roads
Connecting the townships—
To have him appear at the door,
Brisk as a dwarf, glittering with victorious malice,
Notched and elfin as a frosted oak leaf,
Bitter with nut gall—
To have him appear and ask with bland contempt:
"Any final directions?"

## Thelma Ehrgott

I may have wavered a little,
And yielded a little at times to you,
Spoon River.
But never did I lose the vision wholly,
And at last I had the vision wholly,
And saw with clearest eyes the truth:
Divinity never clothed what you did to me,
Nor what you thought of me.
Divinity never clothed your customs or rules,
Your laws, nor even your creeds!

## Nathan Kost

Rum, Romanism, and Rebellion:
Wine, the ritual of beauty, and resistance
Of those who wish to rule you,
And still make you bear the mistakes of that rule;
Forbidding to you to bear the mistakes of ruling yourself.
All of these profoundest truths
Snatched from me by the mob, by ugly catchwords.
Hurry, O Earth, towards Alpha Lyra!
Burn up in some erratic flame,
Leaping a million miles from the sun!

## Aristide Proulyx

What is this talk of the wages of sin,
And flying from wrath to come,
And pointing to Lucius Atherton
As a case of decay from lawless lust?
Did not I fall like an oak
Pulled down by vines, to poverty and death,
With a wife and thirteen children,
And as many grandchildren?
The thing is Nature, not laws,
Not Decalogues!

## Leopardi Erotas

Passer-by! If you are a soul in search of beauty
Know first your strength, and fathom the hate of the world.
For if you find, then lose, your death will be long!
I was a soul who sought
With eagles in their eyries, and by mountainous waters,
The haunts of creatures of wild delight;
And in faiths, and dreams, and sounds;
In springs, in raptured visions of the gods.
Then in the unsuspected light of a face I found!
And in a kiss a deathless pain!
For in that moment the panting hounds and the hunters
Trampled the April silence.
O trembling rushes and ever remembered sigh
Of that evanishment!
With shaking hands I made a pipe,
And sang and sang;
And wandered singing beside dead seas
That mourn to sinking stars!

## Van Raalte Ramey

How do you regard yourself as good, Spoon River,
When you spent all your power
In breaking wills, and depriving people of happiness,
And forbidding the gayety of horse races,
And the fun of wrestling and boxing,
And the pleasure of light-hearted wantoning,
Prompted by nature and the emptiness of life;
And the friendly saloon,
And counted all this to righteousness?
And yet at the same time pursued me
With mockery and insult,
Until my self-esteem was gone,
And my pride, and my power to do my best.
This was the course by which you said to me:
"Thou fool!"
And how did you escape the danger of hell fire?

## Burton Fairman

Deluded souls! Do you know why you make bequests
To libraries, hospitals, churches?
You fancy yourself on a balustrade up there
Overhearing the reading of your will,
And the exclamations, "What a great soul!"
It will not be so.
Your thrill is now
Fancying yourself listening then.

## Elza Ramsey

Do you know what makes life a terror,
And a torture, Spoon River?
It is due to the conflict between the little minds,
Who think life is real,
And who therefore work, save, make laws,
Prosecute and levy wars—
Between these and the big minds,
Who know that life is a dream;
And that much of the world's activity
Is pure folly, and the chattering of idiots.
But did they not break through the shining light
Of my dream and keep me conscious
Of their laws and jails?
Yes, even to this spot!

## *Clifford Ridell*

Nothing outside of it,
Boundless and filling all space.
At one with itself, being all,
And bent to no will but its own.
Changing forever, but never diminishing.
Every part of it true to the whole of it,
However a part of it wars with a part of it.
Disharmony comes from two, not one.
Friendly with itself, for otherwise
It would perish.
Is it good or evil? But how evil,
Since there is nothing with which to compare it,
And make it a blunder, a mistake?
Without disaster, having no fate, being fate itself.
Unutterable unity,
Eternal creation,
Changing, but never destroying, not even me!

# Genevieve Faulkner

You shall have your wish, it is written.
And indeed you can, though nothing is worse.
It's like the shortest way to a place:
You miss the sights of the longer way.
It's growing a rose to have your wish,
You snip the smaller roses to grow it.
It's giving all your love to a friend,
You miss so many friends by the giving.
And here was my wish: to marry my children
To sounding names in places afar.
And I had my wish for one in Russia,
For one in Italy, one in France.
And then to see them I had to wander.
And so I wandered, until their welcome
Cooled, and I found I had make their lives
To the loss of mine. Why Bridget Brady
Whose daughters married railroad switchmen
Here in Spoon River, and feasted with them
On Christmas day, and New Year's day,
Was happier than I.

## Bradford Randolph

The kingdom of heaven is like unto a man
Who worked a field, believing at last
That it was unfruitful,
And so deserted the field
When it was really prospering, and would harvest.
That was I, friends of Spoon River,
Who spent years in the wooing of a heart.
Then in a moment of doubt and discouragement
I turned away from that heart
At the very time that heaven was mine,
And all in ignorance that it was mine!

## Miriam Keith

To love is to give
Admiration and understanding.
I have given my understanding to some,
And my admiration to others;
But never both my admiration and understanding
To any but Bradford Randolph,
Who gave me admiration, but not understanding.
Hence we were lost to each other.
What subtle combinations of spirits must be
To unite hearts, however they strive!

# Nevill Hone

I shall be more than two thousand years forgotten
When the world will look upon
This Bible created and Bible dominated era
Of two thousand years
As the most monstrous period of time,
Tangled, wounded, tortured, imprisoned
By a thousand falsehoods and slaveries.
I who was most gifted for happiness
Was unhappy, because of these things,
Knowing all the while
That happiness is the only good,
Happiness is the only end.

## Norris Kernan

To the god Jesus what sacrifices!
Chastity, the scrubbing of floors, care of lepers
Celibacy, hair shirts, poverty, death in life.
Martyrdom, faggots, crosses, wild beasts.
Self-crucifixion, long years of lonely watching.
But there is a god more terrible than Jesus,
To whom Heine, Shelley and Poe
Gave everything of heart and brain,
Of love and life,
Amid dishonor, want, disease,
Hatred, contempt of the world,
And without hope—
O merciless Apollo!

## Reuben McCardell

As I was physically unfit
I could not pass the Army tests,
And so escaped the war.
Then I took my place with the ten million Americans
Who never learn to write an intelligent letter;
And the fifty million
Who do not comprehend free government,
And the half of the State legislators
Who never get beyond the grammar school.
Who will save this people from themselves,
Seeing that they have ears and hear not,
And eyes and see not?

## Alfred Nelson

Here by your side, mother, adored soul!
As my body grew from the milk of your breast,
So did my genius grow by your watchful wisdom,
Who guarded my time and strength
Against the vanities and anxieties of the world.
That love, instead of the love of mistress or wife,
Whose beauty, pride, place in the world
I had been seduced by sex to celebrate,
Was the sun and dew of the flower of me.
Then the ecstasy of your eyes
Who looked upon the growing work of your hands,
And whose love did not pluck me
To adorn yourself for one triumphal hour . . .
Here by your side, mother, adored one!

## Saul Kostecki

As a boy I made sand piles
On the shore of Spoon River,
Watching them cave and slide on one side
As I patted them and built them up on the other.
This was my own nature at last.
I strengthened my will
Only to cave in my sympathies.
I cultivated love only to be hollowed with credulity.
I thought of myself and narrowed my vision.
I did for others and suffered in fortune,
And in faith in man.
I doubted, and the good side of me slipped.
I believed, and was broken by betrayal.
How could I keep the sand pile of my nature whole,
And pointed like a pyramid to heaven?

## Anson Stressel

You who denounced me for living in the heights,
And called me as hard as the rocks of the peaks,
Cold to the humanities, as you termed it,
And out of touch with you, Spoon River. . . .
Do you know what would have happened
If I had descended to the soggy plains of your life?
You were always afraid of me.
But if I had come among you, you would have bound me,
And vulgarized me, and then ignored me.
For putting on that tenderness,
For the lack of which you censured me,
You would have destroyed me!

## Orson Warwick

The laws are made upon superficial judgments,
And by shallow minds.
The moralities are prescribed
Out of fears, envies, hates,
And out of empty ideals.
The dangerous woman is not the harlot,
But the wife;
Man is the weaker, not the stronger vessel.
Wine is not a mocker,
But a magnifier of reality.
Denial is the mocker,
And the kingdom of heaven
Is the delusion of the starving.
Friends! Facts are the food on the table,
Ideals the mottoes on the walls of the dining room . . .
Follow the facts!

## John Lamore

Make a fight to feed the brood,
They will down you if they can,
No matter what happens to the brood.
But desert the brood! And they will rail at you;
They will say they would have helped you if you had stuck.
They are a crooked and cruel gang, passer-by,
And the only way to beat them
Is to be strong enough to rob them first,
And store away what you have taken!

## Estella Weston

After estrangement and separation,
Here am I, Estella Weston,
And yonder is Thomas Endicott,
Who should have been my husband.
Have you ever seen a cruel boy
Pinch the tails of sleeping kittens
Until they scratched and bit each other?
So it was with us in Spoon River.
They would not leave us alone, and they put
In our mouths such lies about each other;
And they worried us and wearied us,
Until our nerves went tangled and broken,
And then we quarreled and parted!

# Nathaniel Grieg

You never can tell
What one of the many thousands you knew
Will be the one to meet you;
Nor the soul dynamics that life has set in motion,
Which will inevitably cause the one to meet you:
Once at a dinner I met a woman
Whom the hostess cut with leveling irony.
I saw this woman's tears
And followed her to a little parlor,
Where I took her hand and said, "too bad!"
I never saw this woman before that,
Nor after that.
And yet as I entered here
She was waiting to receive me.
Do you not see that there are laws and secrets of spirit
As wide and deep and mysterious
As the laws and secrets of germination,
Of springs and material births,
Of tides and winds and stars?

## Seidel Loveman

Your curses against life seem at first
To repel or keep at bay,
And to effectually mock and character
Life's disgust, and pain, and defeat.
But at the last, you who curse
Will be as the boy who whistles against the darkness
And terror of the storm.
Curses are a mocker and a raging.
And when you have cursed your fill
You will be but a dead snake,
Whose dried and broken skin
Lisps to the air a simulation
Of its dying hisses!

## *Sterling Sucher*

Now that I was a name in the world,
After thirty years of obscurity,
And my drama was hailed by everyone;
You marvelled—I saw it in your eyes,
That I sought with such persistent hunger
Fellowship and association,
And lingered wherever I could find them.
Here I was on the heights at last—
But my chum of thirty years was there:
Old Loneliness still held my arm,
As I stood on the peaks, and was known at last.
And yet the habit of seeking stayed;
And I sought as I had sought of yore,
And I was as lonely as before.
How strange at this time to die, you thought.
But I was alone, and as hungry, too,
For love as ever I was, my friends—
I had lived too long a life of seeking
Ever for it to leave me!

## Meredith Phyfe

Come now! You supercilious detractors of America
As a land of aridity, without stories and myths,
Without romance, without epic material:
Did not Brigham Young found as good a religion as
    Henry VIII,
And build a greater city than Henry VIII ever built?
Are not the Forty-niners, the Oregon Trailers,
The Daniel Boones and the Sam Houstons
As full of pictures as the Crusaders?
Did not the Fathers, so called,
Accomplish as much as the knights of the Table Round?
Are not Carrie Nation and Mary Ellen Leese
As mad and significant as Joan of Arc?
Was any war of Europe
Bloodier or more momentous than the Revolution,
Or the Civil War?
And why dream about Peter the Hermit
With John Brown under your nose?
Is Robin Hood a fitter subject for ballads
Than Jesse James?
And have we not had Dowies and Schlatterys and Bryans
By the score,
With every variety of religionists
From Shakers to Holy Rollers?
What do you want for irony, satire or pathos?
Is there not every thing here, grotesque,
Absurd, tragic and heroic?

Have you not seen in your own life
More than twenty states acquire more than two million
    people,
And several cities acquire more than that number of souls,
And dozens of cities acquire a half million or more?
Have you not seen mountains climbed, railroads built,
Iron and coal mastered,
Over this vast stretch of restless, crazy humanity?
Is the Woolworth building nothing,
And St. Peter's everything?
Think it over,
You supercilious dreamers of dead days!

## Sophie Wassner

There are spend-thrifts of fortunes,
And mismanagers of fortunes,
And there are spend-thrifts of gifts,
And mismanagers of gifts.
I was dowered with personal beauty,
With grace and brillancy of mind;
Yet I married the wrong man,
And chose the wrong friend,
And bought the wrong house,
And made my home in Spoon River
To my undoing,
Till at forty-five I awoke to see
That all my life was wasted,
And nothing was left to me but to grieve
To the day of my death!

# Leander Morphy

A. D. Blood had prohibition;
And Tennessee Shope the Bhagavad Gita;
And Thomas Rhodes the making of money;
And Lydia Humphrey the Holy Bible;
And Rev. Wiley the thrill of revivals;
And Lucius Atherton lust for women;
And Harry Goodhue the great millennium.
And I a realist for living
Built my dreams on morphine.

## Nathan Suffrin

Jail would have killed me
Except for my cell mate, Henry Luthinger,
Who had been there often before,
And knew how to soften the walls and bars,
And how to be a friend in jail.
So when they let me out,
I knew at last that life is a prison.
And the best that a man can hope for it
Is a cell mate wise and good!

# George Hogg

I was blamed for selfishness—
But who makes it a fault?
The have-nots make it a fault, with their squeals
Following the sow of Riches.
The whole morality of feeding others,
And giving all to the poor
Is made by the hungry, and the failures.
But has money no privileges?
It takes to itself the right to stop its ears,
And fold its arms
Against the squeals of runts!

## Balfour Tozer

You read from a book, I read the rocks,
Friends of Spoon River,
I studied the gravel, sand and mud,
Limestone, shale,
Around the hills of Bernadotte!
And found that chalk is but the remains
Of little things that lived.
So while you talked of the fall of man,
Sin, salvation and faith,
It came to me that men and women
Live their life and dissolve in death,
And make a chalk for gods who study
Soul geology!

## Manuel Lanphier

For a lamp to burn perpetually
Before the picture of soul consecration
There must be the wick and the oil,
And the hand to tend them.
Have you who have seen the lamp
Before the picture
Considered these things?
And did you think of me who passed among you,
Always with the light of consecration
In my eyes?

## Nels Mysky

Carve for me the shape of a griffin,
With the neck and the head of a one-eyed snake,
And a one-eyed snake for a tail.
Read in the book of Genesis
The mysteries of Phoenicia and Greece,
And think it over: What was the snake?
What was the apple?
Why did Eve eat the apple first,
And how did she eat it?
And what was the shame for their nakedness,
After eating?

# Percival Foreman

Morality, the good life—very well!
Do you know what is the most sensitive nerve?
The money nerve.
It accounts for all customs, all behaviors.
Do you wish to make a man change his politics?
Pinch the money nerve!
Do you wish him to get religion,
Or to write different editorials or books,
Or to lecture on acceptable themes?
Pinch the money nerve.
Would you break down his will from a clean dedication
To a new life of truth?
Pinch the money nerve!
Do you know of ten men who have not been broken to
    harness
By pinching the money nerve?
You knew me, eh?
Well, I cleaned up by pinching your money nerves—
I kept items out of my paper for a consideration—
Then I lived as I pleased!

## Cowley Rider

I worked and bought a house for her,
I showered my benefactions upon the children,
Who were like her, and worked against me—
They weren't my children at all.
When I awoke at sixty years
To find that they had my property,
And the children were hers, and their spouses hers,
And I was left to a little room
In the house I earned, and the rest of the world
Was dead or strange to me:
The wages of goodness is Death!

## Geoffrey Kemble

We are far off, far away,
Friends of Spoon River,
And never come at the bidding of the psychics,
Spiritualists, workers of the planchette.
There are the ashen stalks in the fall;
The gray ectoplasm of vines and plants,
And the snow white wraiths of thistles and floating down,
Which mimic the fluttering leaves of June,
And stir, and dance, and bend, and nod!
Are these ghosts of anything?
Or are they themselves now turned to nothing,
But still obeying the listing wind?
Even so memories of love that is gone,
And faces vanished, and hands that we touched,
Come back as voices, lights and sounds;
Come back as faint thin echoes of amaranthine words,
Along the stir of desire,
The zephyrs of unutterable longing!

## Joseph Meek

Did I not see the righteous scowls of the Circuit Judge,
And read the bitter exaggerations of the editors,
When proof was made that union sluggers
Were paid five dollars a day to slug the scabs?
And yet in this same court,
And amid the silence of the press,
And with the aid of the same judge
I was ruined in my little business
By the canning works in a suit in equity
Whose lawyer was paid five hundred dollars
To get me out of the way!

## Ernest Waverley

First it seemed to me
That man cannot serve two masters: God and Mammon;
So I lived by that belief, serving God.
And in the stress of that high devotion
I began to break, and I chose the opposite text:
Render unto Caesar the things that are Caesar's,
And to God the things that are God's.
So I fell on the rock and was broken;
And it fell on me and ground me to powder.
And I say unto you that even from the Bible
One must have the mind to pick the true from the false,
And to know the path for the true or the false that you
    choose.

## Watt Fulgene

Was my offense worse, friends of Spoon River,
Than the offense of Judge Shuman?
I robbed the robbers of the brewery,
Lawlessly taking from them what they had lawlessly taken
From the lawless brewery.
And Judge Shuman, who at that very term of court,
Had appointed a new receiver for that brewery,
And a new set of attorneys for the new receiver;
And had taken from the old receiver and his attorneys
All their fees, perquisites and peculations,
And given them to the new receiver and his attorneys,
As a reward for honestly exposing the old receiver
And his attorneys. . . .
This Judge Shuman sent me to prison
For robbing the robbers!

# Louis Kimberly

Consider, passer-by, what revealments,
Of good and bad came forth
Through the fall of Thomas Rhodes' bank.
Look how it showed the strength of the wife
Of the cashier George Reece,
And the continuing power of Pope the poet,
Dead two hundred years, who wrote:
"Act well your part, there all the honor lies."
What currents played around that event,
Testing out who was steel and who was lead!
And I say that nothing happens in life
That is not good, and a contribution
To the fund of wisdom for future lives.
And consider me, lying latent, called forth
To build a wiser and juster realm
Of money for Spoon River!

## Bayard Gable

I was seventy-three, and she was thirty;
And I had desire and strength for desire,
Enough to last for a year or two or three.
But above all I could have given her wisdom
Out of the richness of age.
And for myself I needed companionship,
The tenderness of a friend,
The sympathy of a wife.
But she drew back, she wouldn't marry me
For fear I couldn't give her desire for desire,
Not even perhaps for a year or two.
O Nature, mocker of man's soul come to flower!
You mow with a cruel scythe all growths
Where the blossom of passion is failing,
Or has vanished!

## Maurice Westerman

My great sin, passer-by,
Was my life as I lived it, made up of daily sins
All a part and in key with the sin of my life.
But my sin was of the head, not of the heart.
Wherefore I say to you the living:
Educate the head, not the heart.
Jesus did not say that his crucifiers lacked in heart,
But, "Forgive them Father, for they know not what they do."

# *Gottfried Fruchter*

Nods and smiles, and gifts and dinners,
And credit, and all good things when all is well. . . .
That is friendship, that is song and blossoms
When the sun shines.
But when the clouds come and the rains drift,
Are there songs, are there blossoms?
Do not smiles grow wan, are not eyes averted,
Are not gifts withdrawn, and are not doors
Softly closed?
Do you not stand in the garden house for shelter,
Counting the broken stems of blossoms,
And taking from your pocket faded petals
Scented with the winds of June hills?
Outside, perhaps, is a sun flower
With head erect still, bowing to you gently.
And within, crouched in a crevice of wall and roo,
Is a swallow, hiding with broken wing,
And eyes that search your eyes!

## Sylvester Wilson

You will go on forever, Spoon River,
As you have always gone:
Treating each other as if life would last forever,
And that happiness could be taken
After revenge and business were cared for.
You will go on breaking the wills of each other,
Forcing ideas of life upon each other,
Making laws, trampling delight,
Making plans for years to come.
You will go on so, blind to the fact
That property, just property
Is at the bottom of all this illusion
That life will last forever!

## Piersol Sutton

What did you care, Spoon River,
Whether the gardener Ostrum
Raised your cabbages in a good season or bad,
Easily or amid difficulties,
Fighting insects and cutworms,
Or free of them?
What you wanted was the vegetables,
Which were no better because they were hard to raise.
So it was with my book, Spoon River.
Illness, poverty, sorrow and soul fatigue,
Cutworms of doubt crawling in darkness of mood,
And the rabbits of daily worries, strive as I would,
Concerned you not at all in the end.
The question was, is this a book?

## August Giese

Is the Nebular Hypothesis a guess?
Is the Origin of Species a guess,
And the Descent of Man a guess?
But is not God an hypothesis,
A guess?
And which is better, to say God made us,
And made the world, and stop with that,
Or to search and explain the processes
Of life and the world,
Without taking any hypothesis
As a cause uncaused?
Here I lie who guessed wrong as to this,
This couch of clay!

# Edward Weibel

I had two wives, fellow citizens:
The first kept me in possession of myself,
And more clearly myself,
By being so different from me.
The second was my affinity:
She poured herself into me,
And she drew myself into her
Until I was lost:
Like clear water that becomes muddy water
When mixed with muddy water!

## Isabel Freeling

How I tempted the snake into the garden,
Then flew for safety into the tree,
Leaving my father to fight the snake!
And how I made enemies for my brother
To live and strive with, while I departed
Abroad where they could not reach me!
Geniuses without themes,
Here is a theme for a thousand pages!
Show how I burned my garbage
In the yards of parents and relatives,
And left them nauseated, choking,
While I was breathing the air of the Alps!
And show how I planted bombs malodorous
Which exploded after I left.

# Jean Guerin

Would you have kept your strength, Voltaire,
And your invincible biceps,
If you hadn't wielded the ax and the sword,
But instead had been made to scratch for fleas,
Bat flies and hunt cooties.
Suppose they had marked you for this annoyance:
Every morning a bulletin about the Sunday School,
And the Missionary Society,
And a request for money for the minister,
And a request for money for the Law and Order League.
And you couldn't smite them,
Because the newspapers guarded them,
And if you turned upon them with satire higher up,
They only glanced at you mildly,
Forgiving you, returning no word,
Still sending the bulletins—
What would you have done?

## Israel Gobini

Deny it if you will, fellow fools;
Each one of you is made up of cells,
And the cells are made up of atoms,
And the atoms are made up of electrons and nuclei,
And the nuclei of electrons and protons,
And their whirling and clinging in a life business
Is determined by fire, electricity.
That's all, that's a man!
What else? God? Immortality?
How do you get that except the electric ether stirs?
And is that stirred, does it stir itself?
Or is it God, the Thought and the Thinker too?
However, take a breed of people,
Persecuted and compelled to explain,
And create a hope in order to live at all;
So the ether stirs, and makes Jehovah, who seems outside
The electrons and protons.
And all the while he's just the reflection of netted light
Flickering on the face of the cliff
From the running brook sun-smitten.
How do I know this? Jehovah died
When men no longer needed Jehovah,
But needed God and made him!

## Aaron Greene

Who are the gods?
The gods are the thrice distilled principle of history,
Of which all the matter of fact has been interpreted.
Who are the gods?
The gods are the pure quintessential of understanding,
Judgment, wisdom,
From which passion, prejudice, ignorance,
Have been strained—
To these I appeal for justification!

## Margaret Moynihan

A new freedom, breaking with eager roots
The tough old sod of the past!
But what is the flower? And what the use of the sky
Better than last year's blossom used it?
Was it for what I lived and did
That Hester Prynne and Hetty Sorrel,
And Tess of the D'Urbervilles loved and suffered,
And Flossie Cabanis flouted the village?
Or was it that I might love and kill
The sprouted seeds of a planted life,
Just for the sake of a selfish freedom,
And a great career?
Refusing marriage, and lying here
Not used, abandoned, nor even shamed,
But shaming rather the lover I fled,
And dying rather than have the child,
Which I didn't want, as I didn't want
A home or a husband!
You were right, Walt Whitman, to say to the States:
"Make provision betimes for insane asylums,
You are in a way to create at last
A nation of lunatics."

## Cleanthus Trilling

The urge of the seed: the germ.
The urge of the germ: the stalk.
The urge of the stalk: leaves.
The urge of leaves: the blossom.
The urge of the blossom: to scatter pollen.
The urge of the pollen: the imagined dream of life.
The urge of life: longing for to-morrow.
The urge of to-morrow: Pain.
The urge of Pain: God.

**THE END**

"The best poems in *The New Spoon River* are superior to any in the first book; they are more desperate and violent, more tragic. . . . These confessional monologues of tragic existence are closer to the worlds of Theodore Roethke, Robert Lowell, and Sylvia Plath than to poems by any of Masters' contemporaries."
—Willis Barnstone

Now available for the first time in many years, *The New Spoon River*, Edgar Lee Masters' continuation of his famous *Spoon River Anthology*, describes in 322 micro-biographies the spiritual and physical disintegration of a small American town.

As in the earlier volume, the lives and relationships of the citizens are interwoven, but in this sequel Edgar Lee Masters takes an even sharper view of the town's response to the encroachments of industry and urban life, the mechanical civilization that at once fascinated and repelled him.

He epigrammatically describes the people

*(Continued on back flap)*